BABY ROBBERS

By
HELEN BRADLEY HALL

Helen Bradley Hall

A
Helen Bradley Hall
Novel
Copyright © 2012

ISBN 978-0-9658140-7-2
LCCN 2012904296

Editor: Ray Glandon

Cover design: Bradley's Publishing

Bradley's Publishing Co.

Helen Bradley Hall

About the Author

Helen Bradley Hall was born August 24, 1973. With her high school diploma in hand, she enrolled at The National Institute of Technology, now known as Everest Institute. In May 2006, Helen graduated from NIT with a grade point average of 97.6, receiving her Medical Assistant certificate. While attending school, Helen had written her second book, titled, *The Battle Within.*

Helen obtained a job working in a doctor's office as a medical assistant and was later diagnosed with Lupus in 2006, but she continued to work in the medical field. In 2007, Helen ended her career in the medical field but continued her career as an author. She currently attends AIU online, has obtained her associates, and is working on her bachelor's degree in Forensic Science, with plans of eventually obtaining a law degree. This is her fourth book, and she is working on many others. Helen continues to stay in the Lord, giving him the glory and honor for all that she has done, acknowledging that she is nothing without the Lord Jesus.

Special Thanks

First, I want to give thanks to my Lord Jesus Christ, without whom none of this would be possible, and I acknowledge that it's his will that I was blessed with such an honorable gift to share my inner most thoughts with the world. I would like to thank my husband and children for supporting me again as I embark on another writing journey. I'd like to thank my mom for her support. To all that purchased my book, I send a special thanks to you the reader. I acknowledge that without you, the reader, I am only an author, but with your support, I am able to continue my writings and perhaps, help others.

Prologue

The book you are about to read is based on a true story. The names of the people involved have been altered. The events are real. Some of the areas and locations involved have been changed.

No mother should ever have to endure the nightmare Dahlia was about to face. Many will read this book in continuous judgment of the mother, Dahlia. You must read the whole story to know the truth.

We must realize that being a single parent is a tough job, and as a parent, it is our duty to protect our children by any means necessary.

Many say some things only happen in the hood. Most people realize anything can happen anywhere. Some people consider Inkster, Michigan the hood; it could pass for such. The hood is the heart of the city whether east or west. Inkster is a suburb in the metro Detroit area. It is near Westland, Canton, Redford Township, Garden City, Dearborn, and Dearborn Heights.

Crime exists everywhere. When and where a crime takes place does not discriminate. It just happens. You read it in the paper; you see it on the news. One would have to be sheltered to think crime can't happen because you live in Bloomfield Hills or any other suburban area. It's life. We are not exempt because we live in the suburbs. It is the same as individuals that live in the hood. No matter what we do, whether good or bad, we still suffer hardships and problems. You can be a Christian or a non – believer, and you will still encounter the misfortunes of this world.

ONE

Talandas Amid Heirloom was born July 20, 1990, the day the Detroit Pistons won the championship. Dahlia, feeding her baby, watched the game unfold and the celebration that followed. "You can't touch this" by MC Hammer was the celebratory song for the champions. It was printed on T-shirts for all to know that Detroit held the basketball championship. Dahlia, happy to be a mom, even though she was young, did what she had to do to raise her child.

As time went on, Dahlia and Manure had two more boys, Woodrow and Valentino. When Talandas turned 3 his mom and dad divorced. Dahlia filed for child support and was alone raising three boys. The divorce was Dahlia's choice, choosing to end an abusive marriage from her son's father. She was tired of the fighting and did not want her sons raised in an abusive home.

Elated for once in her life, she had peace. No arguing or fighting, no womanizing man in her life. She was focused on raising her boys. She didn't believe in bringing just anyone around her boys; she wasn't looking for a dad and definitely didn't want someone coming into her house trying to run things. She was an independent woman and wanted to stay that way. Dahlia was holding her own, not asking her ex husband for a dime. Although she filed for child support, his broke ass paid none of it, but she still maintained without it.

Trying to make a way for her sons, Dahlia had some struggles but managed to come out smelling like a rose every time. She had some wilted petals, but they revived over time.

Dahlia lived in the city of River Rouge from 1993 until 2001, on Campbell Street between Jefferson and Schaefer. For eight years she resided there and was ready to move because the owner of the home was dying from cancer and she knew the house would wind up in probate.

In the summer of 2001, Dahlia brought her children to Detroit and found a five bedroom home on Cedarlawn, in the Wyoming and Plymouth area. Talandas began to fraternize with some kids in the neighborhood that were not good. She warned him and forbade him from communicating with them. Talandas still tried hanging with them anyway. Dahlia told Talandas, "If you get in any trouble dealing with them and a cop or anybody shows up at my door, I am gonna whip your ass cause I done told you." Talandas wasn't a troubled child as far as the law was concerned, but she knew if he continued to hang out with those kids, it would all change.

Sometime during the summer 2001, a man knocked on Dahlia's door and her son, Talandas, was standing beside him. The man spoke, "I caught your son and these young men in my yard; they were trying to steal my motor bikes."

Dahlia angrily flung open the screen door saying to Talandas, "Didn't I tell you, if you got brought home with this nonsense, I was tagging your ass? Get in here, now! Upstairs!" Turning back to the man, she spoke, "I apologize sir. My son has never done this before, but trust and believe me, you won't catch that little nigga back on your property again. Now these other little niggas ain't my problem; they live down the street." As soon as Dahlia closed her door, she grabbed her belt and stormed upstairs to Talandas's room. Not asking any questions, Dahlia started whipping his ass saying, "Didn't I tell your little ass if you got brought home, you belong to me? I done told you to stay away from them little bad ass kids. You like stealing? This is what happens to thieves in my house." The whipping stopped and Talandas rubbed his behind, mad, but what the hell could he do? He had been warned. Talandas knew Dahlia wasn't holding up any ass whippings if he needed one, but he tested the waters and drowned that day. He stayed away from those kids.

School was starting in a month, and Dahlia was ready for school to start back because Talandas was again slipping in the streets. He was choosing the wrong kind of folks to call friends. He was having trouble in school, always getting suspended, and Dahlia just didn't understand that. She was the kind of mother that went to every parent/teacher conference and stayed on her kids about an education, but Talandas just couldn't function in school, it seemed.

On a cold, snowy day, Dahlia's phone rang. A voice on the other end said, "Ms. Heirloom, this is Mrs. Daggers, the principal at Drew Middle School. We need you to come pick up your son. He is being suspended for running in the hallway." Dahlia hung up the phone with no reply and headed to the school.

Walking into the school's main office, she hears Talandas saying, "What are you talking about?"

Then a man's voice says, "Turn around and put your hands on the wall." After hearing that, Dahlia followed the voices as they kept talking. She finds her son and a man searching him.

Dahlia stepped in between the man and Talandas

asking, "What is going on here? Who are you to be searching my son? He's only being suspended for running in the hallway."

The man said aggressively, "Ma'am I am a police officer ...

Dahlia interrupted, "I don't care about you being no damn cop; how the hell you going to search my son for running in the damn hallway? That doesn't require a cop searching no damn kid! Now get your hands off my son." Out of the blue, an arm wrapped around Dahlia's neck trying to bend her backwards, but she flipped the individual off her back.

It was a man getting up off the floor, yelling, "Ma'am, you just assaulted an officer!"

Dahlia angry yelled back, "You did not identify yourself as an officer. Your big ass came from behind and grabbed me in a choke hold and got flipped. Assault my ass!" Throwing her hands behind her back, she uttered, "Talandas, go home now, you are done here, and you dumb ass cops, this shit won't stick."

As Dahlia was being escorted out of the office, parents stood and clapped saying, "Girl, that's right, they wrong as hell! Yep, we heard everything. That was some bullshit." That evening they cited Dahlia with disorderly conduct and fined her $50. Dahlia contacted her mom and told her where her stash of cash was so she could come and bail her out cause the dumb ass cops would not go into her property to retrieve her money so she could make bail. Twenty minutes later Dahlia's mom showed up, and she was bailed out.

Drew Middle School expelled Talandas from their school indefinitely because he had several suspensions from that school and Dahlia preferred Talandas attend another school anyway. Dahlia was angry with Talandas because she had no choice but to homeschool him. She had to go through Lansing to do so. She homeschooled him for an entire year, hoping to get him back on track. When he returned to school in 2002, he was in his correct grade but in a different school. Talandas attended Noble Middle school. It was a long time before he got suspended.

In 2003 Dahlia met a man by the name of Ripley. Ripley and Dahlia met on a chat line and talked on the phone privately for 8 weeks before he was allowed to come to her home. Dahlia and Ripley set a date for him to rendezvous with her. It was on a Thursday night, in July. Dahlia prepared dinner for her children and made them go to bed around 10:00 p.m. An hour later Ripley showed up. Dahlia wasn't concerned with him being a nut job because he was a gentleman on the phone, and when they met face to face, he was a complete gentleman, very mild mannered. They laughed, talked, and had a great night; they were enjoying each other's company. Before long, it was 3:00 am. Ripley, being the gentlemen he was, stated, "I had a wonderful time with you tonight, Dahlia; however, I must be going, sweetie, I have to work tomorrow. I'll call after work." Kissing her on the cheek Dahlia opened the door, walked onto the porch with him, then made sure he was safely inside of his car.

Dahlia and Ripley developed a relationship over time. She could not believe there were still some good men out in the world. She had been with Manure from the tender age of 15 until she was 22, so all Dahlia knew was his terrible ways. Ripley and Dahlia became the best of friends. Ripley came to escort Dahlia one night when he accidentally met Dahlia's eldest son, Talandas, as he was entering the house. Dahlia's sons were on their way to their grandma's house to stay while Dahlia went on her date, and her daughter, Tyler, was gone to her dad's for the weekend. Dahlia and Ripley had been dating for 4 months, but he never saw Dahlia's kids in person. He only saw their pictures on the wall. Two months later, Dahlia finally let Ripley meet her other two sons, Woodrow and Valentino. Dahlia's daughter, Tyler, he was not permitted to meet yet, but in due time he would.

Two

Dahlia wasn't very friendly. She would sit on her porch and check out the scenery. All was silent. For years, Dahlia just sat there, waving hi and bye to her neighbors. In 2004 Dahlia began to kick it with only one neighbor, a woman named Tracy. She lived down the street, and she was cool. They became very close friends. It took Dahlia three years to become cool with someone in the neighborhood.

It was the summer of 2004 when Dahlia was sitting at her computer, typing up her second book that she was going to publish the upcoming year. She could hear her children outside playing. She had her dining room window open so she could hear and the blinds open to see. All of a sudden, she heard a yell and a cry. The neighbor, a little boy who lived down the street, was holding his face walking home crying. Dahlia asked her son, Wood, "What's the problem?"

Wood angrily spoke, "That little boy slapped Tyler." Dahlia politely went to talk with the young boy's mother. She knew there would be a problem just by looking at the woman. The boy's mother laughed after Dahlia told her what just happened.

Dahlia kept her cool and said, "You think that's funny? He slapped my daughter. How old is your son?"

The woman spoke, "He's 10." Dahlia spoke again, and this time her anger was pronounced, "Dig this here, baby girl. That little girl your boy slapped, she's five."

The woman interrupted, "Yeah and that big boy jumped on my boy." Dahlia interrupted, saying … "And he did what he was supposed to do, which is to protect his little sister. But I tell you what, keep your boy down here and away from my kids and my kids will stay down there where they always been. Do you hear what I say? I've been living here for three years. I've never had a problem, and I am not about to." Dahlia turned, heading back home. Once she was there, she warned her kids, "Stay away from that little boy because he's going to be a problem." That same little boy kept coming down to Dahlia's house to play with her kids, but she would politely send him away. Three weeks had gone.

It was a hot summer day in July. Dahlia was inside watching television and heard Wood outside yelling, "That's my sister!" Dahlia quickly went outside. What she saw angered her. There was a girl in Wood's face pointing her finger in his face, chastising Wood. Dahlia flew off the porch.

Once she was close enough, Dahlia pushed the woman by the forehead with her index finger, backing her away from her son. Stepping in between them, Dahlia emphatically asked, "What's the problem baby girl?"

The woman spoke snobbishly and loudly, "I want to know what went on down here."

Dahlia, pissed off, spoke calmly, "First of all little girl, you come down here checking a kid. He has a mother, me. You should have been knocking on my door talking to me, not my kid. Secondly, I don't have to explain a damn thing to you, so you can calm the fuck down. I don't like the way you came down here."

The woman spoke, "Bitch, I'll kick your ass."

Dahlia, standing only five two and a hundred pounds, stepped in the face of the five foot five, one hundred and ninety pound woman and said, "Here it is, whip it. Make it do what it do baby. There is nothing between us but boobs and air, bitch. I just stepped to you raw, now what?" The woman backed up. Dahlia shook her head with a smirk on her face and said, "I didn't think you wanted this ass."

When the young lady's step father grabbed her, she got tough all of a sudden, yelling, "I'm going to whip your ass."

Dahlia calmly said, "I just stepped in your face, we were nose to nose, breast to breast, and you did nothing. You got punked. Go home before you get beat down." Dahlia walked on her porch and sat down, leaving the eighteen year old running her mouth.

An hour later car loads of people pulled up at their house down the street. Dahlia saw them coming her way. She politely went inside and grabbed her aluminum baseball bat and gun. As they approached, she warned them, "If you all step on my porch, I'm splitting the first nigga head that get here first." All those people kept yelling, selling wolf tickets. Dahlia spoke again, "You all are some punks. You all down here yelling. It's six against two, me and my bat. All you got to do is take the first step and your head will be cracked, coma style." The 18 year old yelled out, "Your son shouldn't have jumped on my little brother."

Dahlia spoke, "Bitch, what! Are you stupid, he should have got his ass tore out the frame like he did for slapping my five year old daughter. That's a girl, he a boy. It will happen again if your little brother touch her again, and you can't do shit about it, bitch."

Angry, the 18 year old said, "You come down here on

the ground. We're all going to kick your ass."

Dahlia flicked her cigarette and went on the ground and said, "Now what all you bitches going to do? If you all don't mind being put in comas, I don't mind putting you fools there. So come on, swing, just one and you all going to get it." They kept yelling at Dahlia doing nothing. She stood there listening to the dummies yell useless insults. Smoking her cigarette with a smile on her face, she thought, they standing here getting all out of breath yelling, all that energy to yell. If I were to just lose it right now, they dumb asses would be too out of breath to run or scream. She began to laugh loudly. They didn't carry out their threats because they knew Dahlia had some screws loose, and she wasn't scared. After Dahlia saw they were on some bullshit, she walked back up on her porch with her baseball bat dragging the ground. She sat down, flicking her cigarette butt into the crowd of yellers. The entire neighborhood stood there watching to see what was going to jump off. Those idiots wouldn't leave from in front of her door. After looking at them for another ten minutes, she decided to remove them. Dahlia searched for bricks. As she found them, she stacked them on her porch. While stacking them she said, "All six of yawl got punked by little old me.

It's four women and two men. You men ought to be ashamed down here with some females, acting like some Pussies. You men got pussies because you down here trying to punk a woman, and you all got punked by a woman. Get the hell from in front of my house with that malarkey; you all aren't stupid. You're not talking about nothing." She jumped behind the pile of bricks and began hurling them at the same time she spoke, "Didn't I tell you dumb motherfuckers to get from in front of my house with this bullshit!" They all began to run. One of the men picked the brick up. When he did that, Dahlia quickly grabbed her gun from under her shirt, aiming it right at him saying, "If you throw that brick back I'm going to blow your fucking head off." He dropped the brick, and they all left. Securing her gun back inside the house, she went back outside to sit on her porch. Forty minutes later, the police came. They went down to the troublemakers' house first. Dahlia knew they were coming to her house. Dahlia thought to herself, I can't believe those bitches called five - o when they were at my house. She calmly waited for the police. Ten minutes later, they came. The first question the crooked officers asked, "Where's the gun?"

Dahlia angrily spoke, "It's inside my house."

"Is it registered?"

"Yes it is."

"Ma'am, we're going to need to see your registration for your gun. My partner will go in and get it."

"No, he's not going in my house to get nothing, I'll go get it."

"Is it loaded?"

"Hell yeah it's loaded, nigga. This is the hood. I'm a single mom who lives alone with four kids in an ignorant ass neighborhood."

"Ma'am, we're going to have to have our guns drawn if you go get it." With a frown on her face she said,

"Man, that's a bunch of bull. You don't have to have your gun on me. I am not a cop killer or a criminal." Dahlia walked inside making all her children go to bed. She grabbed her gun and registration and headed back outside. All those punks were next door. Placing the gun on the porch along with the registration, one of the officers retrieved the gun. Checking to see if there was a bullet in the chamber, and there was, the officer then unloaded the gun while the other officer looked at the registration and asked Dahlia what happened. As she was talking, those clowns were standing there yelling at Dahlia, and the cops had to intervene. They knew then who was the problem.

They gave her registered weapon back, and the officer said, "Ma'am, careful with this thing."

Just before they left, Dahlia said, "Officer, if they come back down here on my property, you will be back with a coroner's truck next time, not one but six, so please tell them to leave me alone now."

The officer's went where they were standing and told them, "If you all go back to that lady's property like that again and she shoots, she has a right to defend herself. There are six of you all. That will make anybody use force. Besides, that's a little lady, what were all six of you all down there for? If you call again, I will take you all to jail. Dahlia called her family to let them know what just jumped off, so if anything happened, they would know why.

The next morning, Dahlia and her mother, Cecily, walked to the store. They had to walk past those clowns house. The 18 - year – old's mother spoke, "Hey! How are you doing, Dahlia girl!"

Dahlia snapped out, "You got the nerve to speak to me after you and your family tried to punk me and got punked yourselves. I'll blow your face out, bitch."

Cecily interrupted ... "By the way, bitch, let my daughter call me one more time telling me you motherfuckers came back down to her house, and I'm coming back over here with cars loaded with nigga's and we running up in your crib and we ain't doing no talking."

The woman, scared, told her son, "Go get the phone, Burt."

Cecily spoke again, "Call whoever you want, bitch. Call Tyrone, because you heard what I said. I'll be at my daughter's house. Yawl some punks. Yawl let this little lady punk all six of yawl. But you knew the score; that's why yawl didn't lay a hand on her." Dahlia and her mother continued their walk to the store. All was quiet for a couple of days, and Dahlia did what she always does. She walked past their house to take her daughter Tyler to school and picked her up the same way.

The children went back to school in late August. Summer vacation was over. In the second week of September, on a hot Tuesday afternoon, Dahlia walked to pick Tyler up from school. The hood was quiet. All that was in the streets were the crack heads and hookers trying to get a trick or a hit to start their day. On the way back Dahlia noticed from the corner that her troublesome neighbors were all standing out on the porch of their house. Dahlia had a feeling they were going start some shit. Dahlia always walked the closest to the street while walking with her daughter. But this time, she placed her daughter there just in case they wanted to be stupid. They would not get to Dahlia's daughter before reaching her. Grace said to Dahlia, "Yeah you come back down here again, Dahlia, I'm going to whip your ass."

Dahlia angrily said, "Tyler, go on home and lock the door, I'll be right there." Grace continued running her mouth. Dahlia waited until her daughter made it home and inside. Dahlia headed towards their porch. Grace began to back up. Dahlia, now in Grace's face, yelled, "Look bitch, don't threaten me. I ain't running. Come on, Billy bad ass. Do what you said. I done told you motherfuckers I ain't no punk. I am on your shit now. Do whatever you bitches gonna learn today. One of yawl gonna get a good ole fashioned ass whipping. You gonna fuck around and get your ass kicked up and down Cedar-lawn, and you ain t going to want it when you get it. I am trying to be cool now, bitches. I done told all you." Dahlia paused, looking Grace firmly in her eyes. Grace stood there looking like she saw a ghost. But she didn't move or say anything else. Dahlia laughed and said, "Yeah, just like I thought. You a punk, too. If you ain't talking about scrapping, don't talk to me. I'm telling you, dude, yawl better stop. I'm getting you though, all yawls. If any of yawls walk past my crib, I'm jumping off my porch and whipping yawl ass. And you want to be men down here that are truly broads I'm busting at yawl, rata tat nigga." She walked off their porch and headed home, fed up with their madness. For the rest of the summer, none of them, male, or female, walked past her house. They weren't crazy, but they knew Dahlia was.

The summer was coming to an end, fall was making its grand entrance, and it was still warm. Dahlia, pulling up in her driveway, saw those bad ass kids of the family she had been beefing with on her porch playing on her porch furniture. She made those kids go home. Hours later, Dahlia sat on her porch and noticed three of them coming her way. With her scalpel in her back pocket, she stepped down on the sidewalk in front of her house meeting them there. Clark, yelled, "Yeah, they are about to whip you something terrible."

Dahlia stood there with her hands in her back pockets and said, "I am not worried about that at all, Clark. Yawl been saying this for months, and nothing yet." She continued to take drags off of her square, patiently waiting their approach.

Once they were there, Clark tried to push Grace, his girlfriend, into Dahlia, saying, "Whip her ass yawl."

Grace, out of fear, jumped back not touching Dahlia at all and said, "Nope Clark, don't be pushing me into her."

Dahlia, with a smile on her face, said, "Smart girl, Grace. Now, what you want, Bernadine?" Still with her hands in her back pockets, Dahlia spoke once more, "Your sister - in - law here, she smart, Bernadine. She scared as she should be. But you, Bernadine, you stupid. You going to mess around and get an old school ass whipping. I done told you, girl. You 18 and I am 31, go on and play with someone your age, gal because if I put my hands on you, it's going to be vicious, so go! I am trying to be civil, but you clowns are making that difficult. Why niggas always gotta make other niggas go nigga on them? This shit ain't cool yawl, we neighbors act like it. Oh! By the way, I am saying this for the last time, and the last time only, last warning yawl for real, please stop coming down to my house with this motherfucking bullshit, and your brother who is a 10 year old boy, my daughter is a five year old girl, he should have got his ass tore out the frame like he did. Let me explain something to you motherfuckers, she has three older brothers. That was only one that whipped his ass. Next time that little motherfucker touches my baby girl, all three of her brothers going to whip his ass at the same time. Yes, they are older than he, and I will be the one calling that order in on that. Now get the fuck from down here." Dahlia was infuriated because these dummies would not let this shit rest until somebody got stretched out on the block. Dahlia had four kids, two with disabilities. She was not trying to catch a case for some damn dummies, but they were not going to keep coming down to her house, either. See, Dahlia wasn't the type to call her peeps over unless it was really popping. Niggas had to have been touched for the family to be called, but you better believe they knew about the dummies down the street. They were just waiting for Dahlia's call. They were ready and down for whatever.

Grace, the smart one, spoke while staring at Dahlia. "Bernadine! You better leave that woman alone. She ain't scared and she ain't playing. You going to mess around and get your ass whipped good messing with Dahlia. Are you looking at her? She ain't flinching or nothing. She waiting for one of us to touch her, and it ain't going to be me. Clark, she ain't afraid of you either. This woman going to end up shooting you. Man, didn't all six of yawl come down here and she chased yawl away? Man! Yawl better leave this woman alone, for real." Grace turned and walked away. Clark and Bernadine followed. Once again they came to her house for nothing. She was getting fed up with their low - life asses coming down to her house with drama. Dahlia felt like they were disrespecting her kids because that's where her kids laid their heads. Dahlia was very protective of her children because of some things she had been through in life. She would risk doing time if someone harmed one of her children. Dahlia was a female/male figure in her household, and it had been that way since she had separated and divorced from her three sons' father. Believe it! Dahlia stood her ground against male and females because she didn't have a damn choice.

That night Gavin and McGowan had pulled up. McGowan yelled, "What's up Dahlia? I'll be over on the porch in a minute." Nodding yep, in response, an hour later McGowan came over and lit a blunt. He knew something was wrong. He asked, "What's up Dahlia? You seem angry."

"Dude, I want to kill one of them bitches down the street, man."

"You want to kill who, man?"

"Them bitches, Clark and them, they keep coming down here with all that madness. It all started with that little nigga, Morris, slapping my daughter, Tyler. So my son, Wood, in return, waxed old dude, sent Morris home crying. Three weeks later his Elsie the cow looking sister, Bernadine, bring her ass down here, called herself checking Wood. She got checked by me, and it's been beef ever since."

"The men came down here too, Dahlia?"

"Uh huh! But as you see, they weren't talking about nothing; they got punked by little old me. It was six of them, and it was me, my bat, and my gat." McGowan was laughing his ass off.

He said, "Yeah, they was some punks. When I see Clark I'm firing on that nigga because how you going to be down here on some woman's beef."

Dahlia laughed, saying, "Whatever, I don't give a fuck what you do to that clown ass nigga. It's all good. I got it under control. Believe that … they ain't crazy." McGowan was smoking his blunt and Dahlia, her cigarette.

Nightfall came. McGowan, Carol and Gavin were sitting out on Dahlia's porch enjoying the summer air, listening to music. Suddenly, they see the tree leaves moving fast, then a loud pop, pop, pop. They quickly turn the music down and hear the popping noise again and the zipping noise through the trees. They knew it was gun shots. The shots were coming off of Plymouth road. Twenty minutes later they all walk to the gas station. They noticed in the parking lot of the gas station gun shell casings and broken glass. At that point Dahlia realized she needed to get her kids out that neighborhood. There had already been murders and shootouts, among other things. It was time to go, she thought. She began to look for a house outside of the city of Detroit. She wanted to go to a better school district and neighborhood for her children.

December came and Dahlia was still searching for a house. A week before Christmas, on a Thursday, Dahlia walked up to the corner gas station. When she walked in, Bernadine was there at the counter, talking to the manager about a job. Dahlia grabbed what she came for and headed to the counter to pay for it. When Bernadine turned and saw Dahlia, she got scared and ran out of the store. Dahlia, paying her no attention, paid for her things and left the store. Dahlia, walking through the alley way, heard a car behind her. Turning to see who it was,

Dahlia grew angry because it was Bernadine playing games once again. Dahlia turned and kicked the grill out of her car, then kicked it once more, this time fucking up her radiator. Bernadine waited for Dahlia to be a far distance away before she got out to assess the damages to the front of her vehicle. Dahlia, calmly walked home. Bernadine drove down the street slowly, rolled down her window, and yelled, "You kicked my car and tore it up! I'm going to kick your ass for real!"

Dahlia laughed, saying, so do something for real this time. I dare you!" Bernadine accelerated down to her mom's house. As usual, Dahlia wasn't worried and kept walking.

When Bernadine made it down to her mother's house, she jumped out of her car yelling, "That bitch kicked my car and tore it up. Come on yawl." They all headed down to Dahlia's. It was boot – mouth, Bernadine, her brother, Clark, Grace, Clark's girlfriend, and their mama, Drusilla.

Bernadine, yelled,

"Come on down here, Dahlia."

Dahlia was four houses away from home with a smile on her face when she spoke, "Trust me, I'm coming, I don't know why you rushing to get your ass kicked. You ain't going to want it when you get it." Trucking along through the snow,

snow still coming down, Dahlia reached her house. Bernadine had her fist balled up.

She was mad, but scared, "Grace, don't let her hit me with that bottle she got in her hand." Grace responded, "Bernadine, I done told you, I ain't got anything to do with this. That's between you and Dahlia." Dahlia had a smile on her face and stood there. Bernadine slapped the plastic bottle out of Dahlia's hand and pushed her.

Dahlia spoke, "Bernadine, is you crazy girl? You was worried about that plastic bottle that couldn't hurt you. You should have been worried about these keys." Dahlia grabbed Bernadine by the hair yanking her closer to her height. She began punching Bernadine in the face with the keys. The only sound heard was the clank of the keys before talking began. Clark and his mom, Drusilla, were talking at once.

Clark asked, "What is that clanking noise?" Drusilla had eyes so big she looked like she just had a drug she shouldn't have had.

Drusilla chanted, "Whip her ass, Bernadine! Whip her ass! Oops! Oops! She is whipping your ass, Bernadine! She is whipping your ass!"

Clark says, "You can't tell your family we helped her

fight you." Dahlia, with her back against her house, steadily whaled on Bernadine while her eyes were on the other three. Bernadine was struggling to turn Dahlia's back towards her family so she couldn't see if they tried to jump in. Dahlia made sure her back stayed up against her house, so she could still beat the shit out of Bernadine while her eyes were on Bernadine's three family members standing there.

Drusilla said, "Dahlia is whipping your ass, Bernadine! Dahlia done whipped your ass, Bernadine." Tearing away from Dahlia, with Dahlia allowing her to, Bernadine was humiliated, mad, and feeling like an ass. She walked away whimpering in tears, with her family in tow. Drusilla says, "Ooh, your face is bleeding, Bernadine!"

Dahlia, laughing her ass off, yelled, "Yeah, Merry Christmas, bitch. Wrap that present and put it under your tree. Santa left you an ass whipping. I told you I was going to give you an old fashioned ass whipping, girl, and your mama stood and watch. Drusilla, you need your ass whipped, too." It was Thursday, a week before Christmas. Bernadine received a special wrapped gift from Dahlia for Christmas. Dahlia knew they were going to call the police, so she sat at her window until she saw a patrol car. Walking on to her porch with a square blazed, she stood and waited for them to come down to her house. Dahlia wanted to bust her upside the head again because how was Bernadine going to call five - o when her dumb ass invited that ass whipping. The officers finally made their way down to Dahlia's house, getting her side of the story.

Drusilla came rushing down the street yelling, "Officer, take them both to jail, they need to cool off."

Dahlia angrily spoke, "You stood down here and watched your daughter get her ass beat. She should go to jail because she had no business down here in front of my house."

Bernadine came down in front of Dahlia's house to talk to the police. She asked, "Officer may I look for my keys in her yard?"

The officers yelled, "You told us you weren't down here. You lied to us."

Dahlia laughed and said, "See officer, this is what I'm talking about. They come down here get what they asking for and lie about it. Officers, don't let her come in my yard to look for nothing." Dahlia walked away and began to look in her yard. She found some Lee – press - on nails that belonged to Bernadine. Dahlia picked them up and flicked them at Clark saying, "Take your sister's fake Lee – press - on nails and get from in front of my house, and she better find her keys before I do because if I find them first, they are being dropped in the man hole." After that, Dahlia had no more problems out of them. She had to earn her respect by whipping ass. Dahlia never wanted to go there; she did what she had to do.

Dahlia was still looking for another house. The whole time she remained on that block she didn't have any more problems with those folks down the street, Bernadine or her family. In March of 2004 Dahlia finally found a house that was in a decent area, so she thought. She had her boyfriend, Ripley, looking for a house for her in his area or nearby. She was looking, too. She found a house in Inkster, Michigan, she was interested in, and she had Ripley go check it out. It took awhile to get in touch with the landlord of the property, so she kept looking on her own.

It was May of 2004 when Dahlia finally got in touch with the landlord. She made an appointment to look at the inside of the house. It was smaller than what she was used to, but she took it. Dahlia figured it was better than the city. Dahlia went home to finish packing up the things she wasn't using at the current time and left the essential things they used daily until they were ready to move. Dahlia was moving in mid June, a week after her children were due to be recessed from school for the summer vacation. She set it up that way because she hated moving her kids during the school year.

Three

𝕿he day came for Dahlia to move. With the exception of the neighbors from hell, all the rest of her neighbors were sad to see her go because she was a good neighbor that stayed to herself. She never bothered anyone. Dahlia warned her children to stay away from the new neighborhood kids because she didn't want any drama in the new neighborhood. She was mainly stating it to Talandas because he was the friendly type that made bad choices when picking friends. Dahlia loved the peace in the neighborhood. They had been residing in Inkster for two months now. Dahlia knew the schools that each one of her children would attend and when registration started. Robichaud high school was the school Talandas and Wood were attending. Tyler had to go to Thorne elementary. Valentino attended a school in Livonia for children with autism and other developmentally delayed disabilities.

In August of 2004 the children were attending their new schools. Talandas was 15, Wood was 14, Valentino was 13, and Tyler was seven. Everything was going smoothly with Talandas. He had not experienced any drama as of yet. Dahlia wasn't getting any calls from the school. The months of October and November exited quickly, and still no trouble from Talandas. When February of 2005 hit, all hell began to break loose with Talandas at school.

Dahlia enrolled at NIT for medical assistant classes. The classes started in September of 2005. She received her certificate and graduated in 2006. Her course was an eight month course, and she had her certificate as a medical assistant. Dahlia made it clear to Talandas that she was going to school so she could better herself and their family and that he was holding down the fort and there was going to be no bullshit while she went to school. Dahlia was excited about embarking on an education one that could land her a good paying job once she graduated.

The school year for the children had come to an end and Talandas began to mingle with some of the kids from the neighborhood. Dahlia knew it would not be long before he would start beefing with kids in the neighborhood. Wood was a good kid; he rarely gave his mom any trouble. He did what he was supposed to in school and he was never suspended. Neither was Tyler. Valentino was disabled and was no trouble at all. Although Talandas was starting to be a problem, he still was a good kid. Underneath all that trouble, Dahlia knew there was good in there. Talandas began to hang out with the kids down the street. Their names were Tike, Paul, and Rico. Dahlia knew they were trouble, but as usual, Talandas didn't listen. As time went on Dahlia began to notice Talandas had a change of personality. He had begun to test his mother.

In spring of 2005, all the kids were outside playing in the front yard. Dahlia was sitting on the porch, then stepped inside to fill her glass up with more pop. Talandas came inside mouthing off to her saying, "When Tyler runs in the street and gets hit by a car, don't come crying to me."

Dahlia noticed his anger and tone and she snapped, slapping him, picked up an iron candle stick holder that stood on the floor and yelled, "Who the hell you think you talking to boy! I watch Tyler! I ain't some neglectful parent, fool! You better watch your tone with me for I bash your face in! You done lost your damn mind talking to me like that, fool! I don't know what friend of yours talks to their parents that way, but that will get you fucked up around here!" With his arms raised in fear of Dahlia doing exactly what she said, he went back outside to play without saying a word. It was a long time before he spoke to her that way again.

In June of 2005, Talandas and his friend, Paul, began to fall out. Dahlia didn't care what it was about because she told him not to get friendly with these kids around here, but he did anyway. Talandas began to have multiple brawls in school, and he began to get suspended more. Dahlia knew he was the problem. There was no other alternative but to let him go through his own problems because he was never going to stop.

In the mean time, Dahlia and Ripley had been together for two years. They began to discuss marriage. They knew they were going to be together, and Ripley adored her children. Talandas was still beefing with that kid, Paul, from down the street.

It was a hot day in June. Dahlia, her windows open, heard a commotion outside. Stepping outside, she saw Paul and Talandas about to engage in physical confrontation in her driveway. Tike, Paul's little brother, spoke, saying, "Here comes Talandas's mother, Paul."

Paul angrily said, "Don't nobody care about his mama, little nigga. He'll still get rocked."

Dahlia spoke, "Paul, you go home, and Talandas you can get on in the house. I told you about these neighborhood bastards. You're going to learn. You just don't listen, but you will one day."

All was quiet. Dahlia was hoping Talandas had a better year this year in school. He had been back to school for two weeks and no problems thus far. September was still fairly warm; it was still summer here in the Metro Detroit area. School had just let out for the weekend. It was Friday. Dahlia had her brother's girlfriend, Lindsey, over to visit. They all decided to go the store. The only ones that were left at home were Dahlia's sons Valentino and Talandas. She wasn't gone but three minutes. Dahlia returned home to Talandas falling into her arms disoriented and bleeding from the nose. Dahlia asked confusedly, "Who did this to you, Talandas?" Dahlia and Lindsey helped Talandas back inside. When she was inside, she saw that her computer desk was broke. Valentino was untouched and there was blood all over her computer desk. Dahlia ordered Lindsey to call the cops. Dahlia asked Talandas again, "Who did this to you?"

Dazed, he answered, "It was that nigga, Paul, his two boy's Mink and Bud." Just as Dahlia was heading down the street, her brother Drawz was driving up the street. He could tell something was wrong with his sister, Dahlia.

Stopping the car, he jumped out asking, "What's up,

sis?"

"Dude, these little niggas ran up in my crib and jumped on Talandas, man."

His eyes grew big, and he asked, "Where was you at?"

"I wasn't at home, nigga, I went to the store, nigga! You think they would have been walking out my crib if I was there, nigga? They would have been leaving by the meat wagon because I would have lost it on them, dude. Somebody was going to be dead." Dahlia and her brother walked down to Paul's house, and wouldn't you know it, that punk was hiding behind his grandmother.

Drawz spoke, "Little nigga, you ran up in my sister's crib? If I catch you on the block, I'm stomping the yard on you young blood." They walked away and headed down to the other little dudes crib that ran up in her house. When they got there, it was a man and a woman on the porch.

Dahlia said, "Your son ran up in my house and jumped on my son with his boys."

The woman interrupted saying, "Hold on. He's my nephew, not my son. He doesn't live here, he just visiting."

Dahlia spoke again, "I don't care what his relation is, hear what I say, and you better get him out this neighborhood because if I catch that fool, I'm going to stomp the yard on little man. He stopped being a kid when he ran up in my crib." They both walked away. When Ripley called on his lunch break, Dahlia told him about the incident. Talandas was taken to the hospital with a contusion to the brain. He healed up just fine. Months later Dahlia and Talandas received papers to go to court. She made Talandas press charges against the one that she could get. He didn't want to; he was talking some street code snitching rule. Dahlia angrily spoke, "Do you have any idea what that street code is fool? It's a code in the street that gets you to take the fall for your buddies' crime or allows someone you know to get away with a crime against you, the individual, while you, the innocent one, rot in prison for something you didn't do. This is their way of getting away with a crime, and considering you a dumb ass, you are pressing charges and that's that. I am proving a point here. And if you fall for that street code jive, you are a damn fool." Talandas did as his mother told him. Paul was given three years probation, and his grandmother had to bond him out of jail for fifty dollars. Dahlia wasn't all that happy, but she took it. She felt he was given a slap on the wrist for what he did.

It was the 2005 – 2006 school year. Talandas had been

at Robichaud high school for a month, and he continued to get into trouble, which seemed like a never ending cycle for him. Dahlia was starting school in two weeks. She was going from 6:00 p.m. until 10:00 p.m. She made sure dinner was cooked and the children's homework was completed. She ironed Valentino's and Tyler's school clothes for the next morning. Dahlia's schooling was a successful endeavor. Talandas held down the fort and did what he was told. He really stepped up to the plate to help his mom make it through school. Everything was calm with Talandas, although he was constantly getting suspended from school.

Ripley and Dahlia had planned to move in together to began their life as a family. They decided to do so in February 2006. Ripley lived only three miles away from Dahlia, so finding new school districts would be easy. The move to Ripley's house was a quick and smooth transition. The kids were excited about the move, and they really liked Ripley; they viewed him as a friend. Before they moved in, Ripley cleared out the two bedrooms to make room for her children. He painted the boy's room the color they wanted. Tyler had her own room. She was the only girl. Everything was great in the beginning. The kids loved living there with Ripley. He was a wonderful man; he treated her children as if they were his own. He was a friend and a father figure. The children began to call him, Pops. They were a family. Talandas loved the friendship and the father figure at first, but he began to change. Dahlia didn't understand because Ripley did things that fathers do with their sons. They had men talks, and they were getting along so beautifully.

It was the summer of 2006. Dahlia had graduated from school and was searching for a job in the medical field. Talandas was still hanging out in Inkster. Dahlia had warned him on several occasions to stay away from that area. Whenever he hung out there, he would come back telling his mom about the gang fights he was in. Dahlia would ignore what he said because he wasn't listening.

Talandas was starting his same routine of getting suspended from Golden City High School. Supposedly he struck a school administrative, a Caucasian female, but she had not a mark from him striking her as she claimed. A school board meeting was held, and the school board decided to expel Talandas.

In October 2006, Dahlia found a job on Middlebelt and 8 mile working for a small doctor's office. She worked for doctors Wong and Romberg. Dahlia loved her job. Her duties were to draw blood, perform x- rays, E.K.G.s and more. Dahlia paid Talandas to babysit his siblings from the time they got home from school until she got home from work. She believed this would show Talandas that an honest pay is better than what he was doing in the streets. Dahlia was no fool; she knew exactly what her son was doing in the streets, but she wanted him to learn this life lesson on his own. He was still going to do what he wanted because he was rebelling. Dahlia would soon learn why her son's personality began to change.

It was a cold winter day in November of 2006. Talandas walked in with some kid in tow. Dahlia and Ripley were on the sofa looking at T.V. Talandas said, "Mom, Pops, this is Ricky. Ricky this is my mom, Ms. Heirloom, and my Pops, Mr. Hessen." Dahlia laughed, then turned her head to see who Talandas was introducing to them. When she turned and saw the young man's face, Dahlia's smile turned into a look of doom.

She said, "Talandas, this kid is a bad seed. I don't like this boy, and if you keep hanging with this fool, you gonna end up in prison. Now, get this little no good thug out my house and don't you ever bring someone like that back up in my house."

Talandas said, "How you gonna dog my man's …."

Dahlia quickly interrupted before he could say another word, saying, "Did you hear what I say, boy? Don't argue with me. Now move!" Ricky was already closing the door behind him, and Talandas followed.

Talandas was hanging tough with this kid by the name of Ricky Stover, whom he knew from Golden City high. Dahlia knew what she saw, and she was to be proven correct over time. Dahlia figured because her son Talandas was going to keep hanging out with this Ricky kid, she needed to know him up close and personal. It was cool with Talandas and Ricky hanging, but Dahlia still had those same old feelings about Ricky, and they just would not go away.

Dahlia noticed Talandas was shooting dice. He would talk about it on his cell phone and would come home with a pocket full of money at times. Dahlia knew her son was not crazy enough to be selling drugs while living in her and Ripley's home, so shooting dice explained where the wads of money came from so far. Checking Talandas about his gambling in the streets, Dahlia became fed up, so she began to think on the next phase of teaching him a lesson. The more she told him to cease his gambling fiascos, the more he refused to listen. At this time he was 16, and he was starting to become addicted to gambling. Dahlia still paid him for babysitting his siblings, but that was all he got from her.

Talandas was becoming more of a problem at home. Everything was happening so fast, Dahlia believed she was living a nightmare. Facing issues with her own health, Talandas was adding fuel to the fire with his bullshit. Dahlia's gastroenterologist referred her to a rheumatologist. She had been suffering from tenderness of her skin and severe joint pain. Three weeks after the blood work and battery of tests, it was determined that Dahlia had Lupus. She was already battling Crohn's disease. She functions on a small intestine because her large intestine almost erupted over 13 years ago.

It was March 2007, and Valentino, Tyler, and Wood had 3 months left before they were out of school for summer vacation. Pulling in her driveway after a long, hard day of work, Dahlia noticed this little blue car parked outside her home. When she walked inside, there was Ricky sitting on her sofa. Sitting there twirling keys around his finger, Ricky said, "Hey, mama!"

Looking at him with displeasure on her face, she asked, "Is that you driving that blue car parked outside?"

He quickly responded, "Yeah!"

Dahlia asked, with concern, "You got a license? And who car you got?"

Talandas interrupted ... "Yeah he got a license, Mama."

Dahlia shot back, "Shut up, boy! I ain't talking to you. I am talking to Rickey."

Rickey spoke, "Yes, I have a license, and that is my auntie car I'm driving."

Dahlia stood there with a grim look on her face sucking her tooth, saying, "Uhuh!" She walked away, and they quickly left.

The spring filled the skies in April. It was a beautiful month so far. The weather was breaking and spring was near. Talandas was dating a nice young lady. Her name was Ariel Lockett, and they had been dating for awhile. She would come to the house and kick it with Talandas's family and have a good time. Ariel's mother would come in and talk to Talandas's parents, and over time they developed a relationship because she and Talandas's parents approved.

Unfortunately, in addition to Talandas's gambling, breaking curfew, disrespecting the house, and God knows what else, he was stealing money out of Ripley's wallet. He had stolen money out of his mom's purse once. His gambling was getting worse. Despite being told numerous times to stay out of Inkster and to stop gambling, he never listened. Dahlia and Talandas stayed into it. She tried telling him something, he'd get mouthy, and she'd slap him. Dahlia didn't allow her children to disrespect her. Talandas was grown in the streets, but he was a kid at home. He lived a double life in a sense.

Dahlia closed the lab down in the doctor's office after she had seen her last patient for the day. She had to make sure all blood work was placed outside in the drop box for the lab to pick up so the results could be in by the next day. It was Friday, and not her Saturday to work, so she was off for the weekend.

After arriving at home, Dahlia showered and began to prepare dinner. Talandas left in that same car that he and Ricky had been riding around in for well over a month. Dahlia knew that car did not belong to Ricky's aunt as he claimed; she knew that it had to be stolen. Dahlia walked into the livingroom peering out the window, watching Talandas enter the car. As they drove away, Dahlia went into a daze when a vision appeared: there was a car in a driveway running. A young boy ran up to the car, jumped inside, threw the car in reverse, and sped off, stealing it. Suddenly, someone shouted, "Mom, Mom! The oil on the stove is popping!"

Dahlia snapped out of her daze, saying, "What, what was that, Tyler? Oh, the cooking oil." Dahlia turned off the stove and began to mix up the ground beef with all her ingredients to prepare homemade Salisbury steak patties. She knew at this moment the car those boys were riding in was stolen. When Talandas arrived home five hours later, Dahlia told him that he was not to have that car around her house. Talandas was about to fix his mouth to argue, but his mother interrupted him before he could say a word, letting him know that she knew the car was stolen. He angrily left.

Later that night, they came back in the same car. Dahlia was awakened by noise, and she could tell it was a bunch of boys. She got out of bed to see what the noise was. When she saw her son, Talandas, and seven of his friends on the side of her house shooting dice, she lost it. She yelled, "How many times do I have to tell you about bringing all these strange ass folk to my house to gamble? This is not a casino. Yawl little niggas got to get up out of here, and Talanadas you get in here and lock my house up." She came back inside lit a cigarette.

Talanadas cleared the crowd out of her yard and sat on the sofa with the T.V. on. Dahlia fell back to sleep but was awakened by a ringing phone at 3:00 a.m. She answered, "Hello."

A rough, deep voice said, "This is detective Branch from Golden City police department. We have your son, Talandas Heirloom, here in custody with Ricky Stover. They led the police on a high speed chase, and the car they were in was stolen. They will be shipped to the Wayne County Juvenile Detention Center."

Dahlia, half asleep said, "Ok, who was driving?"

"It wasn't your son," the officer said. Wood was 15 at the time, so he was able to hold the house down while Dahlia and Ripley went to work that Saturday. She worked from 9:00 a.m. to noon every other Saturday.

Talandas was due to go to court on Monday. Dahlia went to work late that day, so she could see what was going on with her son. Their charges were fleeing and eluding the police, and grand larceny. Talandas's bail was set at $2,500 at ten percent and Ricky's bail was set at $8,000 at ten percent.

His bail was higher because he had a long rap sheet. He was only 15. Talandas was told by the referee that he was to return to court in May for trial. Dahlia didn't bail Talandas out until Wednesday. She let him sit a few more days. May arrived and Dahlia and Talandas sat and waited for their names to be called and for him to speak with his attorney. They sat in the lobby for two hours before they were called into the courtroom. The owner of the vehicle was Mr. Voorhees. He testified first. The prosecutor stood and asked, "Mr. Voorhees, tell us what happened the morning of April 12, 2007."

"I had gotten up at 4:30 a.m. to get ready for work. I work from 6:00 a.m. to 5:30 p.m., so I exited outside to warm up my car about 5:00 a.m., I had come out of the house around 5:15 a.m. and my car was gone."

"Did you see the car taking off?"

"No."

"Did you immediately report the vehicle missing?"

"Yes, I did."

"No further questions."

The referee spoke, "You may cross." The defense attorney for Talandas asked, "So you didn't see who stole your car, correct?"

"No, I did not. Like I stated earlier, I was warming up the vehicle, and after starting the car, I went back inside."

"No further questions."

The defense attorney for Ricky did not cross examine the victim at all. When it came time for Ricky's attorney to call their witness, Ricky's God sister choked. She had nothing to testify to; however, Talandas's attorney called Dahlia to the stand as a witness. His attorney began to question Dahlia, "Where were you the morning of April 12, 2007 around 5:30 a.m.?"

"I was home sleeping, I had to awaken at 6:00 a.m. to get my other three children off to school."

"Was Talandas home when you awakened?"

"Yes, he was home in bed sleeping."

"How do you know he was home asleep? Did you go into his room?"

"Yes, and he was in his bed sound asleep. I had to leave out for work around 8:30 a.m."

"What time do you have to be to work, and where do you work?"

"I have to be at work at 9:00 a.m. I work at a doctor's office."

"What do you do there?"

"I am a medical assistant. I draw blood, perform E.K.G.s, and x – rays, all that good stuff."

"What time does your shift end?"

"My shift ends between 5:00 p.m. and 6:00 p.m. ... sometimes earlier, but I usually leave around 5:00 p.m. On this particular day I arrived home around 5:20 p.m."

"Was Talandas there when you arrived home?"

"Yes."

"Did you ever see Talandas leave in the vehicle in question?"

"Yes."

"Who was with him?"

"Ricky was with him."

"Did you see how they would enter the vehicle?"

"Yes, Talandas on the passenger side and Ricky on the driver side."

"No further questions, your honor."

The referee looked at Dahlia and everyone in the courtroom and uttered, "Your cross, counsel."

"Ms. Heirloom, you stated you were at work from, let me rephrase, you stated you leave for work at 8:15 a.m. and you do not arrive home until 5:20 a.m., sometimes later."

"Yes, that's what I said."

"How do you know Talandas was home all that time?"

"Because his stepfather doesn't leave for work until 1:30 p.m.; and when I call on lunch break, which is noon, Talandas just be getting out of bed. He also has to be there for his younger brother, Valentino to get home. Someone has to stay with Valentino at all times because he has developmentally delayed/autism. Once Valentino gets home, my son, Woodrow arrives home thirty minutes later. And besides, I call periodically all day from work, and Talandas answers the phone. As I said before, he's home when I get there. He knows he better not leave his siblings home alone."

"And why is that, Mrs. Heirloom? Cause it seems as if you're not doing a good job. ... "

Dahlia interrupted, "Excuse me, my son has never been caught in the system like this before. He is almost 17. I think I did a pretty good damn job so far. Do you have children? If not, what do you know about parenting? I am done answering your questions."

She left the stand, and the attorney uttered, "Your Honor, I am not done."

"Oh, yes you are," he replied. Looking around the room he asked if there were any other witnesses. If not, he has made his decision.

"First off, I don't believe for one second, Mr. Stover, that you are innocent as you tried to state in your report while in custody. You were the getaway driver. You, sir, led the police on a high speed chase down a residential neighborhood, and I believe you stole the car because this mother stated her son was home when the vehicle was stolen. Mr. Stover, you will be found guilty of grand larceny, fleeing and eluding. You will be sentenced to six months in the Wayne County Youth Detention Center, and while in custody, a release plan will be developed. Mr. Heirloom, you will be charged with joyriding because the evidence shows that you were not the getaway driver; the charge of grand larceny is dismissed because you did not steal the car; therefore I will sentence you to one year probation. This is your last stop here, Mr. Heirloom. Next time you get in trouble you will be stomping with the big dogs in the county, hear? Court dismissed." Talandas didn't like the probation terms because the probation officer came out to the house once a week to visit and Talandas had to call in once a week. He was due back for a review at the court in six months to see if he would be eligible to be released from probation early.

At this time Talandas was enrolled in Cambridge Academy Alternative school. With probation you have to go to school as well as drop and blow in a breathalyzer. Dahlia was angry because she was going through unnecessary bullshit, all because Talandas didn't listen. Rickey stayed away for a long time after that ordeal, and Dahlia was happy because Talandas was getting his life together and was staying out of trouble.

It was time for Talandas to go back to court for his review. It was June of 2007. His probation officer extended his probation because she didn't like Talandas's attitude. That afternoon when they returned home from court, Dahlia and Talandas got into a fist fight because he was angry about the extension of his probation. Talandas began to curse and totally disrespect his mom, so Dahlia whipped his ass and threw him out by force. She had found out later that day that Talandas had been hanging out with Ricky again for a week. Talandas was now in the streets again. He was just out of control. He continued to gamble, and his attitude was getting worse, as was his behavior at home. Ripley was fed up with Talandas's shit, too, but he let Dahlia handle her son.

Talandas began to lie more. Some of Ripley's money was steadily coming up missing from his wallet, and some of Dahlia's jewelry was missing, too. This was when they began to kick Talandas out of the house for weeks at a time, trying to teach him a lesson. Talandas was beginning to think he was an adult and that no one was going to tell him what to do. The other kids were out for the summer and that was when Talandas really began to crash and burn. The activities that Talandas was involved in while roaming the streets were becoming more violent each time, and Dahlia was soon to see what her son had turned into.

Talandas began to break curfew, and at times he would call his mom and ask if he could stay the night at a friend's house. Sometimes she would grant him permission, and other times she wouldn't. Talandas would get grounded for breaking curfew, and a huge fight would ensue. Dahlia and Ripley would kick him out, and he would call home begging to return. The stealing and the booting out of the house continued with Talandas. Dahlia was fed up and asked his probation officer about counseling services. She believed that Talandas had some deep - rooted issues that he might share with a third party. She got him placed into the Starfish counseling program. It was a nine week program. He went alone twice. Then the counselor requested a family counseling session, and the family went. Dahlia expressed some serious concerns about her son, and so did Ripley. She couldn't understand why it took until he was almost an adult to get in trouble with the law. The counselor could not understand him either.

Talandas continued to break curfew. Dahlia told Talandas, "Every time you break curfew, you will be locked out." Some nights he was left outdoors, and some nights he got home before curfew. Dahlia tried very hard to get her son the help he needed to clean his life up, but he continued to be a law breaker. Dahlia began to think her son wanted to go to prison so he could make a name for himself, you know, street 'cred' is what they call it. She knew at some point she was going to have to let him feel the pain of life because this kid was hell bent on going down the wrong path, but he could not say his mother, Dahlia, did not try or wasn't a real mother. Even when Talandas settled down a bit, it would not be long before he'd be back to his same bullshit, stealing. Same song and dance … Talandas would get put out of the house for weeks and allowed to come back home. She warned him about stealing and that he was going to get put out of the house and not allowed to ever return if he kept it up. Ripley and Dahlia had gotten to the point where they had started to lock their money up in the safe so Talandas couldn't steal from them anymore. Dahlia couldn't permanently put Talandas out of the house until he was 17, so that was the alternative to combat his stealing.

Months had gone by Talandas was still 16, and Dahlia was responsible for his actions. She was beginning to wonder if living with Ripley was a bad idea because her son was causing nothing but problems, and she felt Ripley did not deserve to go through this bullshit drama. The summer solstice had made its entrance. Dahlia was still hanging on to her job, and Talandas had no choice but to continue to babysit his siblings because that was the only way his mother was giving him any money. She knew he was angry about it, but she didn't give a damn. Talandas wasn't her father or her husband; he was only her child. Little did Talandas know his mother was on the brink of letting him go and letting God have his way. She knew he was going down one of two paths: jail or hell was his destiny.

On a June morning, Dahlia headed to work. It was

Friday, and it was not her Saturday to work. She had the entire weekend off. It was hot out already. She adorned a tee shirt underneath her scrubs. She rolled down the window in her car while taking a drag off of her cigarette. Work went by fast. She was glad to punch out and go home to start her weekend. As soon as she arrived home, Talandas grabbed his phone and started to head out the door. Dahlia uttered, "You know what your weekend curfew is. Be here. Don't be on that bullshit. Hear, Talandas? We all going to have a good weekend." She walked away not waiting for his answer because she knew the answer was, yes, Mom. Whether he obeyed was a different story. Dahlia also made it clear to him to stay out of Inkster, and if he traveled to Detroit to be home in time. Dahlia was hoping that her son would get his act together. She tried on numerous occasions to analyze why his behavior had changed. She knew that Ricky was an influence, but it was Talandas's fault for allowing Ricky to have such a great impact on his behavior as an individual.

Talandas left on Friday evening to go to Detroit to visit his girlfriend, and here it was, Sunday morning, and that clown still hadn't called or returned home. Dahlia continued her day because she knew Talandas was going to be home sometime that day, if not, she was going Monday morning to file a missing persons report. Dahlia prepared dinner and everyone sat down and ate. 5:00 p.m. came and still no call from Talandas. 10:00 p.m. came and Talandas came strolling up to the house on his cellular phone acting as if his ass was not in trouble. As soon as he stepped in the house, Dahlia jumped up and backed him into a corner throwing haymakers and yelling, "You done lost your damn mind? Your ass left here on Friday, and here it is Sunday and you come strolling your ass in here." Steadily throwing haymakers, all you could hear was that clown trying to explain. Dahlia wasn't hearing any of his shit. The blows stopped, and she yelled, "Sit your want to be grown ass down. … "

Talandas tried interrupting by saying, "Man! …"

Dahlia swung at him, yelling, "I said, sit your ass down boy!"' Talandas quickly grabbed a seat. He was pissed off, but hell, he deserved it. Standing over him, chastising him for staying out for damn near three days, Dahlia told him that he was grounded.

Feeling like he was grown and he was through with chastisements, Talandas rose from the sofa saying, "Man, I ain't being grounded, and I'm going to see my girl." Dahlia grabbed him and shoved him back to the sofa.

At that time Ripley stepped in and spoke, "Your mom isn't through talking to you, yet." Talandas rose up in Riley's face and a tussle ensued.

Dahlia, in shock, stepped in the middle, and amazingly, with her small stature, she was able to pull them apart, yelling, "What the fuck! Talandas, boy, you have lost your damn mind. You got to go. Get your butt out of here. You wrong and out of order." Talandas kept running his mouth and left the house threatening to come back and do some harm. Dahlia hurled back, "You ain't going to do nothing. Get on away from here because you foul." She slammed the door, she was so angry. She had never seen anything like it in her life. She thought her son would never have done such a thing, but he did. Dahlia began to view her son differently; she began to view him as an enemy. A mother should never have to go through this with a child, but she did. Talandas was kicked out of the house for two weeks. She had an idea where he was, and she was right, he was in Inkster.

Before he was allowed back in the house, Ripley and Dahlia had a nice, long talk with Talandas, letting him know this behavior couldn't continue in their home. They let him back in hoping he would learn his lesson. They made it clear that the next time he was going to be put out and never allowed to come back home. As time went on, Talandas would come home with pockets full of money. Dahlia told Talandas, "If I find out you selling drugs, I'm turning you in myself, so you better not bring it up in here. You see, Talandas, I'm tired of talking. You are just going to have to see it for yourself, and it's ugly. I know you out there on the wild, but you ain't listening. I just pray for your life every day. My prayers keeping you alive, boy, but you keep on running with that Stover kid, and you're going to wind up in prison."

Talandas spoke loudly, "Mama, why you burning bread on me? You act like you want me locked down!"

Dahlia said, "Lower your tone with me, damn it. I'll take that over a burial. I can see you in prison, but I can't see you in the grave." Dahlia was done talking. She searched his room often to make sure he wasn't bringing drugs in her house, around her other three children.

Talandas was so wrapped up in the streets and trying to impress that Ricky kid, he changed into someone his mom didn't know. Dahlia was heartbroken because she always had a good relationship with her children. Heck, even before she moved them into Ripley's house, she sat her children down, and they talked about them moving in with him, and her marrying him. The kids liked Ripley. That was the type of respect Dahlia had for her children. She felt this was their life, too, and it was.

Talandas no longer talked to his mom like he used to; she'd ask him things and he would say, "It's nothing." The 2007 school year had begun. Talandas went back to school in September and by October of that year he was kicked out of Cambridge for inciting a riot. Dahlia was done with his school issue. Once he came home, she said, "You're responsible for finding you a school because I'm through in that department. I home schooled you. Got you back up to speed in your right grade, and what do you do? You go back to school and mess up for the hundredth time. Now you're a grade behind again."

Talandas, angrily spoke, "I can take extra classes to catch up, dang."

Dahlia stepped in his face and said, "That ain't the point. You making it harder on you in school, and if you say "dang" to me one more time, I'm going to slap your face. I done told you, boy, watch how you talk to me. I ain't your friends in the street, got it?" She walked away. Dahlia was at her limit with Talandas and basically washed her hands of him because he was just foul and out of order.

When Talandas and Ricky were walking in the house one day, Dahlia noticed a red bandana hanging from Talandas's pocket. Dahlia asked, "What's with the red bandana hanging from your pocket?"

With a smile on his face, Talandas said, "It's for U.B.N."

Dahlia uttered, "What the fuck is U.B.N?"

"It's a gang, Ma, called, United Blood Nation." Dahlia lost it. She stepped in his face and asked, "What, you in a gang?"

"I sure am." His friend, Ricky had one hanging from his pocket, too.

Dahlia went off crazy style saying, "Take that shit out your pocket little nigga. I don't care what you do in the street, but keep that crap out of my house. You ain't no gangster in here. Ricky, little nigga, you can run yours, too." Dahlia checked in both of their bandanas. Talandas got tough for a minute trying to act out in front of his friend.

He said, "Why are you taking our colors, man? You got to give them back."

Dahlia raised her hand and slapped Talandas, saying, "I ain't giving nothing back. You going to take them? Try it, and I'll bash your head in, little nigga, now what?" Walking towards her door, she opened it saying, "I tell you what, Mister Gangster: your colors on the sidewalk. Get out! Don't come back as long as you gang banging. All you see is that sidewalk that's multi - colored because you going to spend some days looking at that joker wishing you were here." Slamming the door behind him and Ricky, she continued to wash dishes.

Talandas was kicked out for three weeks after that. When he returned home, Dahlia told her son the consequences of getting involved with a gang and how that was not the life to live. As usual, the kid was not listening. He had his head in the clouds. Dahlia began to wonder what else could be done to help this kid of hers. She wanted to exhaust all efforts before she just said, "Fuck it! I tried." She knew the kid was already in therapy. He was ordered to go to the clinic for child study near the Juvenile Detention Center near Forest and Warren.

Dahlia could not and would not allow a dysfunctional home; she liked peace and quiet, and so did Ripley. They were not off into their home being the hang - out spot for all the kids in the neighborhood, and that is what Talandas wanted their home to be ... a home filled with drama every day. Because his mom and soon – to - be stepdad weren't having it, Talandas wanted to cause trouble.

As a parent, you try every option there is to save your child from the streets, but if that child is destined and determined to walk the wrong path, as a parent, you must pray. Dahlia prayed. She and Ripley offered Talandas an incentive to go back to school and get a job. They told him that whatever he saved towards a car, they would match it, but the stipulation was he must have a job, go back to school, and straighten up and fly right. Talandas smiled and said, "You can't get nowhere with honest pay. Honest pay is nothing."

Dahlia was appalled by what he said; she rose to her feet and said, "Look kid, you got it all wrong, ass backwards. Honest pay gets you a long way in life. No one can come and take your paycheck. But that street life, selling drugs. The police bust you. They take your money and your drugs. You starting from the ground up again. Boy I've seen that, lived that many years ago through your sperm donor of a daddy. He been selling drugs since I was fifteen, and he darn near forty and still slanging, so I know about that game, and it's a waste of life and time. He has not accomplished shit from these streets, but you go ahead and do you, because you'll see." Dahlia was pissed off because this kid of hers was a damn fool, and she didn't raise him that way. Now that Talandas had turned to the street life for real, causing terror among neighborhoods with his clan, he was known as Killer Kane.

He was still breaking curfew, fighting with Ripley, and getting kicked out. The fights between those two were getting out of control, and Dahlia had to put a stop to it. Ripley and Killer Kane were involved in a physical tussle. With Dahlia in the middle, words that should have never been said that night were said. Dahlia dialed the police from her cell phone, instead of the house phone because she didn't want to leave from spacing them apart, afraid it was going to come to fists being thrown. Killer Kane was put out, yet again. That night it turned into something ugly between Dahlia and Ripley. They argued up a storm about the dispute between Talandas and him. She was angry with both of them because they were both wrong for the words that came out of their mouths.

Eventually, everything calmed down between Ripley and Dahlia, but Killer Kane was out there living with his friends and still on probation going through therapy. Killer

Kane used whatever excuse he could for the way he was acting. He used an excuse of Dahlia's baby brother, Drawz, going to prison. He went down for armed robbery and received nine and a half years for his participation in the robbery. Dahlia's heart was broken when her brother went away for such a stupid crime. She felt that wasn't a valid excuse for Talandas to be out there being a hoodlum. She tried everything to save her son, but he was stuck in his own way.

For the month Killer Kane was kicked out of the house she was determined to teach him a lesson if he could be taught one. His probation officer, Ms. Rider, was aware of him being kicked out of the home and so was his therapist. During a meeting at Dahlia's home, his probation officer asked Dahlia, "What do you want to do? Do you want to bring him in?"

Pausing and thinking about his issues, she said, "You know what, Ms. Rider? Call me weird, crazy, or whatever you want to call me after I say what I am about to say. This kid think the juvenile system is a joke or a game. He is in a gang now, so he claims. No telling what else he is doing out there in the streets. Sending him through the juvenile system is futile for him because it would not do any good. This young man seems to think he a man, and he will get in trouble again. At that time he will be sent through the adult system, and you guys are obsolete at that point, right?"

With a smile on her face, Ms. Rider responded, "Yes."

Taking a deep breath, Dahlia said, "Well, let the adult system handle him because he in the juvenile system, and he still acting as if he ain't on paper. Let Talandas learn his tough lesson before it's way too late cause he going to keep going until he kill someone or someone kill him. I pray neither happens."

With them both staring at each other, Ms. Rider says, "You know, Ms. Heirloom, you are the first parent I have ever seen that do not coddle their child's wrong doing. You do not make one excuse for your children, and I admire that. You are a great mom. You have done your job. Your son is grown now in the eyes of the law. At least he wasn't in the system at an early age like some kids I deal with." Shaking her head in agreement, she walked away, knowing that his probation officer was going to grant her wishes on how to handle her son.

Talandas was allowed back home after a month. His parents let him know that he was not trusted, and that he had to earn that trust back. He had done a lot of damage, but it could be repaired if he tried. He wasn't due back in court for three months. The referee wanted to see the results of the psychological evaluation from the clinic of child study. At Talandas's hearing the probation term was extended. There was still no early release for him. The probation officer knew he was going to continue to be a problem. Talandas wasn't happy, but what could he do? Ms. Rider did not let the referee know what Dahlia's plan was to handle her son. Dahlia knew what she was doing with her incorrigible child.

Four

𝕴t was 2007 and back to school, Killer Kane was not enrolled in a school at all. He was supposed to be out looking for work, but Dahlia knew he was still doing his street shit with Rickey. Dahlia was planning her wedding for the upcoming year in the midst of Killer Kane's troubles. He continued to be an issue. Killer Kane had an answer for everything. Dahlia stopped talking to him because she was tired of his rebellious ass not listening, and she knew he was going fall flat on his ass for it, too.

Rickey had dropped out of sight again for a spell. It was maybe two to three months he was not seen. Ripley and Dahlia began to give Killer Kane the benefit of the doubt. Underneath that façade of tough gangster, he was a good, young man, just tied to the wrong folks that he allowed to corrupt who he was as an individual.

Ripley and Dahlia knew healing and repairs had to start somewhere. It was a Saturday night. Ripley had a show to play at Jacoby's in Downtown Detroit. Although he had a really good job, his favorite pastime was playing and writing music, which he still does today. Ripley is a talented musician who takes pride in his music. Dahlia had rounded up three of her friends and her mom to see his band play live. Dahlia was having a great time that night and tied one on. Tired from the late night and a bit buzzed, they arrived home around two in the morning, which is a typical musician's life when they play out. When they arrived home, Killer Kane wasn't there with his siblings. Dahlia angrily asked Wood, "Where is your brother?"

"He went to the store," Wood said. Just as he said that, Killer Kane came strolling up to the house. Dahlia knew something wasn't right, but she blew it off, trying to give Talandas the benefit of the doubt. Ripley went down to the basement to put his music equipment way. Dahlia got ready for bed. Lying in bed, Ripley entered the bedroom. Standing there looking down on the floor in a daze, he reached down and picked up a package.

He uttered, "This is strange." Dahlia raised her head to see what he was talking about and got the shock of her life. It was an empty condom wrapper. She jumping out of bed, grabbed the package from Ripley, and flew down to the basement where Talandas was.

Shoving the condom wrapper in his face, she yelled,

"Talandas! Who the hell did you have in my house, not to mention in my bed? Nigga, I know you, you nasty bastard. Why didn't you go in your own room and pounce on that hooker? You gonna take her nasty ass to my room?" Ripley quietly, stood there.

Killer Kane began to lie. "I didn't have anybody in the house, Mama." Dahlia threw her hand up in a slapping motion and took a deep breath because she knew if she hit him, she would hurt him.

She lowered her hand saying, "I know you're lying. You're grounded."

Walking away, Ripley spoke, "You better hope your mother and I don't catch anything."

Killer Kane angrily jumped up, ran behind Ripley, and said, "Look dog, I already told you, I didn't have anyone in here." Then, Dahlia suddenly found another Condom wrapper near the bar with a piece of a left over blunt in her ashtray, and there was a hint of weed in the air. Dahlia flipped out and by that time Ripley and Killer Kane were back at it. Dahlia stepped in the middle, calmed it down, and sent Killer Kane to stay with his grandma, Cecily.

Dahlia continued to pray for the kid because she had

done all she could do. She had whipped him, kicked him out, grounded him, and got him in therapy, but still he rebelled even more. She turned him over to God because only God could fix that child. It was later discovered that Killer Kane had that Stover kid and two hot - tail girls over her house. Killer Kane banged one girl in his mom's bed, and Stover banged the other in the basement while smoking weed.

Dahlia and Ripley were upset because Killer Kane had that going on around his two brothers. She was just glad his baby sister wasn't home. Second, sex in his mom's bed, and he got confrontational when he was cold - busted. Some adults understand that's what kids do. They sneak girls in their house while their parents are gone, but the weed part was just too far out there, and so was fucking in your mom and soon - to - be step dad's bed. One thing about Dahlia … she was a realist. She didn't sugar - coat anything for her children, especially her oldest two boys. She thought that was the worst thing you could do. He was allowed back after awhile. She tried to figure out what to do with that child of hers.

December rolled around. It was three days before Christmas. Killer Kane was now 17, and you still couldn't tell him anything. He still sold drugs in the streets and belonged to a gang. Killer Kane was at home talking to his grandmother that was visiting. The Christmas tree was stacked with presents, and everybody was in the Christmas spirit. He was telling his grandma he was going to get her something for Christmas.

It was a Friday afternoon around 1:20 p.m., and Killer Kane left. Ripley left two minutes later. He wasn't gone even one second and the phone rang. Dahlia answered. "Hello."

"Hey baby, I just wanted to call and let you know that the police are swarming the neighborhood. Something done happened around here." When she heard that, she knew it was Killer Kane they were looking for.

Sadly, she said, "It ain't for nobody but Killer Kane."

Interrupting, Ripley asked, "How do you know?"

Dahlia sighed before answering. "I just have that feeling." After hanging up the phone, she stepped outside to see what was going on, and all she saw were police cars. One slowed down in front of her house, but it kept going.

Hours later, Dahlia got a call from Killer Kane, collect. He was in jail, just like she had thought. He gave her a bull jive story, but she didn't buy it; she knew how he was. She knew she wouldn't know the truth until his court date. During court, she found out that he tried stealing a neighbor's car out of the driveway. He smashed into another neighbor's car speeding out of the driveway and ran into a fence behind him. Once he crashed, he jumped out of the car and began to walk, as if he hadn't done a thing. Yep, he was taking after good ole Rickey Stover. The courts considered him as an adult, and they asked his mother nothing. Killer Kane was in the Wayne County Jail waiting to be sentenced. He was released on five years probation with restitution to pay. He was hit with a driver's responsibility fee, too. Dahlia said nothing, she just let Killer Kane do himself in.

The beginning of 2008 had come. That was the year Dahlia and Ripley were getting married. They were walking down the aisle in eight months; they were set for a September wedding. Even in the midst of planning their wedding they had problems with Killer Kane. Killer Kane had stolen fifty dollars from his grandmother, Cecily, that was supposed to go to his Uncle in prison. An argument transpired on that day when Cecily was over doing laundry. The argument between Killer Kane and his grandmother had gotten way out of hand. Dahlia stepped in and threatened her son, saying, "Little nigga, if you don't watch how you talk to my mama, it's gonna be a serious problem up in here, and Mom, you hush, too, because this fool ignorant, and he got a death wish right now. You know he won't admit to stealing the fifty dollars I gave you to send to my brother, so just let it go. You are keeping it going by arguing at him." As usual, Cecily felt that because she's Dahlia mother and his grandmother, she could say or do what she pleased to Talandas. But Dahlia was not having that from her mom. The argument kept going between Talandas and Cecily when, all of a sudden, Cecily reached out and slapped Talandas in the face. The room stood still for a hot second. Then Dahlia stepped in the middle, and it really got heated. Only seconds had gone by, and Ripley walked in the door coming from the store. He stood there listening for a minute, and out of the blue an argument between Ripley and Talandas began. Moreover, there was Dahlia talking loudly with her mother because of the mess she just created. Dahlia had already got on Talandas's ass about stealing that fifty dollars from her mom's wallet the day it happened, so it was pointless for Cecily to start that huge fight in Dahlia's home. The argument between Killer and Ripley quickly turned physical. Dahlia stepped in the middle. Cecily tried grabbing Dahlia out the way. Dahlia pulled away harshly from her mother and said in a loud tone, "What the hell are you doing? I am not about to let these two fight." Dahlia was angry at everyone now, especially her Mom and killer for being so damn disrespectful. During the fight, Ripley was swooped off his feet and thrown to the ground. The police were called and Killer Kane was arrested. Ripley pressed charges against Killer Kane. That night after Cecily left, Dahlia unleashed a colorful conversation, saying, "Are you out of your mind, Ripley? Are you seriously going to press charges against my son? Yeah, he fucked up, but this is a bit harsh coming from a person that will be his step parent. There are other ways to deal with this shit." Ripley stood his ground and pressed charges. Dahlia understood his principle of teaching the boy a lesson, and in some twisted way, Dahlia agreed with his method because she thought maybe this would wake him up. Still, she was angry. Dahlia said to Ripley, "I will not go and stand by you to send my son to jail, even though he brought it on himself, and I will not stand by my son, either. I am staying out of this. He wants to be grown. Here you go, grown folk shit," She turned and walked away.

    The house had a dark cloud looming over it for a while because Dahlia was still salty behind Ripley and Killer Kane's latest fight that landed him in jail. In the end, he received extended adult probation time and community service. Dahlia was placed in a horrible position, and she felt her son put her there, which he did. Talandas began to shout accusations of his mother placing her soon to be husband before him, when in fact, it wasn't that way at all. Talandas (Killer Kane) was purposefully trying to sabotage his mother's life, all because she wouldn't allow him to control her home, to be in a gang, sell drugs, hang out like he grown, and disrespect her. It all boiled down to the kid being angry because his mom was not taking his shit.

Dahlia and Ripley were more than fed up. Killer Kane was kicked out for good, no coming back. Dahlia, as a mother, had to do it for the sake of the other children and for themselves as well. Killer Kane angrily said to Dahlia before leaving, "I have no respect for you."

Dahlia with a look of doom and anger in her eyes shot back, "Oh, but you will, boy. If you knew what I been through in my life raising you kids, you would have all the respect in the world for me. And this I do know, before this is all over, you will have the upmost respect for me, kid. Do you know who you talking to, boy? I'm a child of God, and this you will know, too, in the end." Dahlia closed her front door as Talandas walked out.

Five

𝕴t was May 2008, and Killer Kane was still living on his own doing what he wanted in the streets. Dahlia hated what she did, but she had no choice. Killer Kane was living in a house on Sunnyingdale in Inkster. It was a house where a Mexican lady lived and allowed kids in the neighborhood, like Killer Kane, to stay. While living there, Killer Kane went to school, surprisingly. He enrolled in Cherry Hill Performing Arts in Inkster. Dahlia fed Killer Kane from time to time and would put a couple dollars in his pocket, but he wasn't allowed back home.

It was warming up. Summer was coming, and people were out wearing shorts. Life looked to be good, but Killer Kane got himself arrested for home invasion and assault, in Westland, Michigan. He was arraigned and shipped to the Wayne county Jail, again. He was due back in court Monday morning. Monday came and he was released, all because the victim didn't show up in court. The judge was angry about that because he didn't want to let him go. Killer Kane went in somebody's house that owed him money, took some things, and threatened to kill them, from what the court said. Dahlia was devastated. Her son had turned into a monster. He allowed himself to be so influenced by Stover that it changed his life completely. Killer Kane went as far as swearing on everything he loved that his boy, Rickey, would never snitch or leave him hanging. Yes, Dahlia knew that was a personal choice that Talandas made to go down that path. No one put a gun to his head to make him turn into a thug. Once they were in the parking lot of the Westland court house, Killer Kane, laughing, smiling and jumping around like an idiot, said, "Oh, I'm a beast. I'm untouchable. The police can't touch me or see me. I'm too cold for them, dude."

Dahlia, pissed off, raised her hand, spun around, and quickly slapped him in the face with all her strength. He stumbled and stopped talking after that slap because he knew he was being an idiot.

Dahlia yelled, "You are a damn fool. If you go before a judge one more time, you through. Ain't no release for you. You jumping around here like this is cute. Nigga this ain't cute. I ought to make your ass walk home. In fact, get to walking, dog." Dahlia walked to her car, drove off, and left Killer Kane's ass walking. She couldn't believe this kid. She thought this is not the kid I raised. Who is this young man?

All she could do was pray for her son. This was like a no - win situation. She was there for him as a mother, but she picked and chose when she did so.

Killer Kane was still living in the house on Sunnyingdale in Inkster. He had mentioned to his mother about his boys and him looking for an apartment because the lady they were staying with was moving. He had been staying there since he was kicked out of Dahlia's home. Through it all, Killer Kane was still going to school. No mother wants to see their child in the street. She thought that would never happen, but she was wrong.

Six

𝕭ack at Ripley and Dahlia's house, peace filled the air. Everyone enjoyed their quiet home: no ruckus to fill the air. Yes, Killer Kane was missed, but they also enjoyed not having drama around. Killer Kane would come by his mom's to eat from time to time and check his MySpace page. The visit from him was nice because at least she knew he was okay. Killer Kane would call his mom periodically complaining about being hungry. "You better get by here the best you can so you can eat or take a plate with you." Sometimes he would, and sometimes he wouldn't. Killer Kane had started going back around his dad, and she was concerned about his activity with him. Killer Kane was old enough to do the street hustles, and his dad, Manure, knew that. Manure had been selling drugs since he was around 15. He had been in the streets for a long time, and still is to this day. Dahlia never wanted any of this for her children, but Killer Kane was determined to be thugged out and roofless. Dahlia knew that her son was out doing things that could and would get him killed if he kept at it. There were two kids that she didn't approve of that Killer Kane was hanging with, and now he lived with those guys.

They were Rickey Stover, known on the street as Rasta and Ugly Z, known on the street as Dirt. There were others that she had heard of but had never seen.

Killer Kane had been going to Cherry Hill Performing Arts for six months. One Morning, Dahlia's phone rang. It was the school. Killer had gotten into a brawl at the school, another gang fight. She simply explained to the Principal that he no longer lived in her home, that it was an issue he needed to talk with Killer Kane about. Hanging up the phone, she mentioned nothing to Killer Kane about the school calling her because she was through talking to him about his life. After that incident, he was still allowed in school. Dahlia was surprised. She knew it would only be a matter of time before he was kicked out because Killer Kane and schools didn't mix. Dahlia felt Killer Kane only went to school to flirt with girls and walk around like he was "the man."

One thing Dahlia always did was keep her kids looking fresh, and she didn't always buy name brand clothing to do so. She took good care of her children. She was the kind of mother that would go without, for her kids to have. Her kids always came first. Killer Kane was the type that had to have name brand. He had expensive taste in clothes and shoes, but

Dahlia got the name brand on sale, and if he didn't like it, she got him nothing.

Dahlia's wedding was approaching fast. June 2008 arrived, and she had three months before her wedding. Dahlia was supposed to be happy, but instead, she had problems and was crying on the inside for her son. Being the strong woman she was, no one could tell because she refused to let anything steal the joy of her upcoming wedding. Through prayer, Dahlia was able to plan her beautiful wedding, even in the midst of Killer Kane continuing to cause trouble.

Seven

Dahlia finished planning her wedding. Killer Kane dropped by one day and told his mom to get him a tuxedo because he was going to be there for her wedding, but she told him no. Dahlia knew deep down inside that Killer was going to be back in jail before her wedding. She was beginning to have dreams about her son being killed. One night she dreamt she rolled up in Inkster to check on her son, and when she got there, the police were everywhere. She jumped out of her car, and there her son laid in the street in a pool of blood with his head blown off. For months she couldn't sleep. It kept her awake for a long time. She was very afraid of it coming true, as her dreams usually did. She had several dreams of her son being murdered, with different scenarios. She prayed unceasingly because she knew death was knocking on her son's door. Even though it was hard to do, she had to let him stay out there so GOD could straighten him out because if she had interfered, surely her son would die.

Dahlia was intelligent as well as spiritually intuitive. She always had a spiritual connection with GOD. Killer himself had a spiritual connection to GOD because he had been in the church since he was three years old, and to this day he still has a connection with GOD.

Dahlia knew something was coming, but she just didn't know what. She braced herself and prepared for the worst. Killer Kane had come by twice in a car with three guys. Dahlia knew they were up to no good. She told him. "Don't bring them hoodlums back to my house. I don't trust them, and if you keep it up with them, you looking at prison time, too." The last time they came by her house, they were in a dark blue, Ford Escape. Dahlia got a good look at one of them because he stuck his head out the window yelling for Killer to come.

Eight

Jt was nine thirty in the morning, June 20th. Dahlia got up at six in the morning and got Wood and Valentino ready for school and out the door. Then she woke Tyler and got her ready for school and out the door. It was now coffee time. That was Ripley and Dahlia's morning routine, having coffee together. It was a peaceful morning, until the phone rang. Dahlia was afraid to answer that call because she had a feeling what it was about. With tears rolling down her face, she answered, "Hello." A deep voice spoke on the other end asking, "Is this Dahlia Heirloom?"

"Yes, this is she, and you are?"

"Ms. Heirloom, my name is Detective Leyster from the Golden City Police Department." At that moment her heart stopped. Dahlia couldn't breathe.

She interrupted … saying, "Yes."

The detective continued. "I'm calling you this morning because I need your help with something. Your son is involved in some things that we can't disclose, but we need your help. We don't want to get your son because it could become very dangerous. All I can tell you right now is your son is considered armed and dangerous, and we need you to bring him in." Dahlia was silent. The detective asked, "Ma'am, are you there?"

"Yes, I'm here. You want me to turn my son in for what?"

"I can't tell you that ma'am because he is considered an adult, and his charges are his responsibility to tell you."

"Come on! I'm not turning my son in and you ain't telling me what for."

"All I can say is that it involves guns."

"Oh my God, he didn't kill anybody, did he?"

"No ma'am, but it's just as bad."

"Its armed robbery, isn't it?"

"Yes ma'am, two counts. Ms. Heirloom, do you know a Rickey Stover?"

"Yes, I know Rickey."

"Ok. Do you know an Ugly Z, a K, a Dari Mitchell, a Mickey, and a Gaither Hill?"

"No, those names don't sound familiar, except for Ugly Z, my son knows him from Inkster."

"What do you think of them?"

"I know that Stover kid. He's no good. The rest of them

I don't know much, but I can tell you this, they're not a good influence."

"Thanks, but we still need you to bring your son in. We have an address for him in Inkster, where he lives with Rickey and K. Dahlia absorbed the talk with the cop, and she knew there was a strong possibility the police would kill her son. She had to turn him in because she didn't want to hear about her son's murder on the news. She thought about it. It all happened so fast.

Dahlia responded. "Look, I'll bring him in, but you better not hurt my boy. If you all hurt my son, it is going to be a serious problem, you hear me? This conversation has been tapped, so be dumb if you wanna, and let your boys know this too, now. I need a contact number, so when he's in my possession, I can call you."

The cop interrupts ... "Ma'am, we would rather pick him up at your home."

Dahlia quickly cut him off, saying, "No, no, no ... you ain't about to run up in my crib with my dog and where my other children reside, honey. We ain't done shit wrong. Yawl better get him how I give him to you or not at all." The detective agreed to a gas station pick up. Ripley didn't know what to say when Dahlia told him what was going on. He was just in shock.

Dahlia, too nervous to drive, called her mom in tears to tell her what was happening. She came to pick her up, and they went to get her son, Talandas. They arrived at the house on Sunnyingdale and pulled up in the driveway. Killer Kane was outside. The woman that used to live there was moving out. She was with another young black man who was helping her move. Dahlia hung her head out the car and yelled, "Let's go, Talandas, now."

Killer Kane walked up to the car, yelling, "Rickey in jail, we got to try to get him out. I got shit to do. Me and the fellas got to get up on some more bread."

Dahlia, in a raised tone, said, "Your dumb ass won't be handling shit if the cops catch you. Fuck Rickey! That's why your ass wanted now. Now get your dumb ass in the car."

Cecily spoke, "You trying to play captain save - a - hoe. Your mama right; you done lost your damn mind." Once he was in the car, they drove off headed towards the gas station on Ford and Inkster. Once there, she got out of the car and went inside. She called the detective that was the head of the case, but the clown did not answer the phone. Dahlia called a second time and still no answer. She went back to the car, and Killer Kane was on the phone talking to someone. Cecily, whispering, almost gave the entire thing away. Dahlia quickly hushed her mom, Cecily, and told her to take her home and to take Killer Kane to her house.

Once Dahlia got home, Cecily drove off. Dahlia called the cops back, and this time they answered. Dahlia told them what car her mom was driving and that her son was in the car. After hanging up the phone, Dahlia began to pray. She was devastated by the whole thing, but it was either turn her son in, let the cops go after her son and possibly kill him, him running and ending up facing more time, or him being killed on the streets.

Dahlia, always told her kids that in a serious charge like that, shut your mouth and ask for a lawyer. The interrogation stops there. Once you ask for legal representation, the cops can no longer question you. A few minutes later, Cecily called, crying hysterically. "Dahlia, they got him. They slammed him down to the ground, girl, and cuffed him. They got us right here on Middlebelt and Ford road." Dahlia began to break down. That was the hardest thing she ever had to do. Putting her disruptive son out of the house was nothing compared to turning her son over for a crime he committed.

Dahlia went inside the house, grabbed her keys, and went to the Golden City police station. Killer's street life was over on the day of his arrest, which was June 20th at 1:00 p.m. It was a domino effect. First Rickey Stover was arrested on the 19th of June. Killer Kane, and Mickey were next. When Dahlia got to the Golden City police station, she asked to see her son. She couldn't until he was arraigned. He was arrested on a Friday, so he wasn't going to court until Monday. The Detective said to Dahlia, "Rickey was released to his father because he was a juvenile." But she knew that was a bunch of bull. Dahlia, looked at the photo lineup of her son, Talandas, Rickey, and Mickey, faces circled, along with three others.

Dahlia looked at the detective and said, "You must think I'm a fool. In a case like this, Rickey can be charged as an adult. Something is fishy, and I'm going to find out what it is."

Dahlia, before leaving the station, yelled so Talandas could hear her, "Boy shut your fucking mouth. Don't say shit until you get an attorney, and I know you hear my big ass mouth." She left the police station in anger because already they were playing games.

That Monday morning, Killer and Mickey were tried together. Dahlia wasn't happy about that at all. Once the arraignment had started, Dahlia found out that they were being charged with two counts of armed robbery and a felony fire arm charge, which is an automatic two year sentence if found guilty. Killer also had a charge of assaulting a police officer. With those armed robbery charges, everyone involved was facing letters (life) in prison. Mickey was let out on bond; he was free up until November 2008. Dahlia was sick to her stomach. She didn't miss a court date for her son. They were bound over for trial. They both decided to be tried by a jury. Dahlia told Killer that it wasn't a good idea. She told him to plead guilty if he did the crime, which she knew he had, even without hearing the evidence against him because she knew the type of folks he was running with.

There was a long process leading up to the trial. There was the evidentiary hearing, the pretrial conference, the pretrial, the jury selection, then the trial. Through the entire process leading up to the trial, Dahlia prayed for the strength to endure because she, herself, was a sickly woman. There were days she tried not to cry, but knowing her son could do life in prison was harsh. Her faith in GOD kept her going.

Killer was now sitting in the Wayne County jail awaiting trial. Dahlia visited her son every Monday, his visitation days. She sent him money to go on his books and wrote him letters. During her visits, she tried not to talk about his situation, but some days it just happened.

One day, while visiting Killer in jail, he began to deny his part in the crime, but Dahlia knew better. She told Killer, "Look here fool. You doing a jury trial, and you know you guilty. You are a fool. They will fry you, boy. Don't you know you can get life, and you think that is going to give you street credibility? Well, it's not!"

He began to argue. "I'm not copping to something I didn't do. My lawyer already said I'm looking at ten years, tops."

Dahlia shook her head, laughed, and said, "Boy, it don't pay to be ignorant and your life on the line. Listen, the judge can give you the max. As long as she's within those guidelines, she can give you life, fool. Doing you has gotten you this far, so keep on until you are sitting here for the rest of your life. Look, I got to go. I'll be back on Monday. Love you kid. Stay out of trouble in here."

Leaving the Wayne County Jail was always a drag because each time she wanted to take her son with her. She felt terrible for turning her son in, but GOD assured her it was the right decision, so her mind was at ease.

Nine

Dahlia's wedding was taking place in three weeks, and she was prepared to walk down the aisle, even during this somber time. She was adamant about not letting her son's life issues destroy her happiness. Dahlia had always put her children first. She did not go back to school to better herself until Talandas was old enough to hold down the fort for a few hours while she attended school. Her wedding was going to happen, and she was going to be happy. She had to put the finishing touches on her day. She had to pick up her wedding dress, the bridesmaids', the matron's of honor, and the flower girl's dresses as well. That was to be done two weeks before her wedding. Ripley picked up all the tuxedos the day before the wedding. Ripley and Dahlia had already had their bachelor and bachelorette parties. Dahlia's mom gave her the bachelorette party, and Ripley's best man, Argon, gave his party. Dahlia really tied one on that night. She really got tipsy, but she had a blast. A great many people came out to her bachelorette party.

Everything was in place and ready to go: the chairs were rented for the guests, and the wedding day was getting closer.

On September 19th Dahlia and her daughter, Tyler, along with Valentino, left the house and would not return until the wedding day. With everything for the wedding packed into the car, they headed to Dahlia's mom's house. All of the women that were in Dahlia's wedding stayed the night at Cecily's house. They all had an early rise the next morning bt still, that night they all laughed, talked, and ate. They were having a good old time. Everyone went to bed late, including Dahlia.

Dahlia and Cecily were awakened by the alarm clock. It was 5:00 a.m. They had to go to the beauty shop for their appointment at 7:00 a.m. The hair salon was not far from Cecily's home. It was in Canton, and Cecily lived in Westland. After crawling out of bed, one prepared the coffee and the other took a shower and got dressed. After they both got dressed, out the door they went. There was still much to do. They were able to relax while getting their hair, nails, and toes done for the wedding. They were in that salon until 8:30 a.m. Once they left, they headed back to Cecily's house to pick up the wedding party so they could go to Dahlia's house and set up for the wedding. Ripley had gone to get the wedding cake to take to the hall. Dahlia made sure he did not see her until she walked down the aisle.

Everything was unloaded from the house. Dahlia and all the women in the wedding party began to transform Dahlia's backyard into a paradise. The arch that Dahlia had wrapped with shear material and some sapphire blue and crème colored roses with a heart - shaped bell hanging from the center of it was placed over a cement block that Dahlia and Ripley were to stand on. The crème colored runner led from the place they were to say their vows to the beginning point of the wedding procession. Along the sides of the runner were sapphire blue and crème colored roses entwined, creating a border around the outside lining of the runner, making it a beautiful aisle to walk down. The grass was filled with crème and sapphire blue rose petals. There were sapphire blue and crème colored balloons that adorned the fence, and there were decorative streamers twisted along the gates.

Once they were done, Dahlia called to see where Ripley was. He was just leaving the hall and headed to the house. It was perfect timing because Dahlia and her crew were on their way to the hall to set up for the wedding reception. Once they were at the hall, they turned that into a paradise, too. The tables were decorated beautifully with glass vases, sand, rocks and floral arrangements in them, all matching the color scheme of her wedding dress, which was Sapphire blue and crème. Once they were done with the hall, it was almost 2:00 p.m. The wedding was to start at 4:00 p.m. They all had just enough time to go back to Cecily's house and get cleaned up and dressed for the wedding.

The time had come. Dahlia was driving down the street and knew it would be filled with cars for their wedding, and it was. The music began to play, and the wedding party proceeded down the aisle arm - in - arm. Dahlia stepped out, and Wood stepped beside her, grabbed her gently by her arm, smiled, and looked at his mom, saying, "You look like an angel, Mom."

Smiling, she responded, "You don't look so bad yourself, Handsome."

When everyone finally saw Dahlia, they were all smiles, gawking at how beautiful she looked. Finally, she was able to see her soon - to - be husband. He looked so handsome standing there waiting to take Dahlia as his wife, smiling at her with such love in his eyes as she walked down the aisle to him. When she arrived, Ripley grabbed her hands, placed them in his, and looked in her eyes.

The Pastor began the ceremony, and when he asked who was to give this woman to marry this man, her three children that were in the wedding said, "We do!" At the end, Dahlia and Ripley kissed to seal their vows and lit their unity candles.

The rental chairs and the arch were put away, and everyone left for the reception hall. Once there, everyone mingled and talked and had a great time. The bride and groom danced to a song by Roberta Flack, "The first time Ever I saw Your Face."

That night was filled with such joy and laughter. Dahlia was happy because she finally found the man of her dreams and married him, but on the other hand, there was Talandas facing prison time. She had that on her mind, too. They danced and drank the night away. The reception went from 5:00 p.m. until 11:00 p.m.

Dahlia's menu for her reception contained: beef ribs, greens, macaroni and cheese, dressing, deep fried turkey, meat balls, corn bread, corn on the cob, potato salad, peach cobbler, and, of course, the wedding cake and ice cream. They served wine and beer throughout the reception. Dahlia gave gifts to her wedding party and gift bags to the guests. An hour before the reception was over, everyone pitched in to help clean up the reception hall. Ripley's parents helped load all the gifts into the car. There wasn't much because almost everyone ordered from their wedding registry and had it shipped to their house. Gifts on their wedding day were cash and checks.

That Monday, Dahlia and Ripley were leaving for their honeymoon. She had previously told Killer before her wedding about them leaving for Las Vegas and when they would return. She made sure she left money for him on his books before she left the state. She knew Killer's trial was coming up, so she thought only about her honeymoon; she just wanted to enjoy her new husband. Killer's trial wasn't set until October, so she had time to unwind before then.

They had a wonderful time in Vegas. Ripley and Dahlia stayed in the Stratosphere near the Vegas strip. As soon as they got there, they checked in, took their luggage to their room, and grabbed something to eat. Then, afterwards they hit the casino floor. Ripley hit the first night. Dahlia didn't but she had fun anyway. They went out front and took pictures, and later that night they walked down to the Circus

Circus casino hotel and walked around. They played some slots there. Dahlia hit for a little change, and they left. Back at their hotel room, they chilled for the night. It was late when they got back.

The next morning they drove up to the Grand Canyon in their rented PT Cruiser. They stopped off in Kingman, Arizona, and had lunch at this little ma and pa restaurant; it was full of antique items, pretty old fashioned, you could say. Eating and enjoying the scenery, Ripley paid for their meal and they left. It was a five hour drive to the Grand Canyon. Smoking hot outside, they rolled their windows down. Dahlia closed her eyes and let the Arizona air hit her skin. After a while, Dahlia opened her eyes and thought, I could live here in Arizona, it is beautiful.

Once they arrived at the Grand Canyon, it was the most beautiful thing Dahlia had ever seen. They walked the path of the Grand Canyon and took pictures. They walked into a little museum there. It was an interesting place that had a layout of the Grand Canyon and stuffed California Condors that once lived there. They drove over the Hoover Dam, and it was beautiful. On the way back, Ripley parked the car and got out to get a couple of pictures of the Hoover Dam. It was dark, so the view was breathtaking, all lit up with lights.

They arrived back at their hotel around six and had dinner at a Chinese restaurant there. They really enjoyed the food. They decided to take the elevator to the top of the Stratosphere. They took pictures and shopped at the stores that were up there. There was even an amusement park ride on top of the building, but they didn't go up. They finally headed back to their hotel room to rest because they had plans the next day, too.

The next morning they had breakfast and hit the streets. They walked the strip, stopping at clothing stores and purse shops. Dahlia loved her purses, so she bought a couple, of course. They walked around the Planet Hollywood Mall; it was huge and unique.

Dahlia was enjoying herself, even though she had some serious issues back home. She was trying to keep it all together, not just for herself but for Killer and the rest of her children as well. There were times Dahlia broke down, but no one knew. She kept it together for the most part. It was difficult. She had to take on the male and female role. She had to be both a father and a mother to her son because he did not allow Ripley to show him what a father's role is all about, which includes handling responsibility and getting one's life in order. Her mind, at times, could race a hundred miles a minute; she was in a whirlwind that only GOD could stop, so she leaned on him.

Their last night in Vegas they hit the casino floor one last time. They both tore the slots apart. Every slot they sat at popped for them. They were feeling good from the Margaritas they had been drinking, boy, they were having fun. They left the floor that night and went home with that Vegas money they won.

On the flight back home, Dahlia thought of nothing. She just wanted to clear her head to deal with her son's problem. They arrived home that Thursday night. She was ready to deal with the nightmare.

Killer and Mickey's trial was set for October 20th. Dahlia's stomach was in knots. She was walking around in a zombie state; she was there but not there. It was three weeks before the trial when Dahlia went to visit Killer at the County Jail. When he was brought into the room to visit, he told his mom that the Detective told him she was testifying against him. She was pissed. Dahlia banged on the glass yelling at him, "What you talking about, fool? I ain't said anything like that. What I look like testifying against my own son? They told you that to get you to talk. I don't know jack, so what I'm going to tell them? Don't come on me like that."

"Oh, I got mad, Mom thinking you was."

"That's sad you don't know your mother. What I did do was turn you in because those cops would have killed you out there. You were armed and dangerous, and if they felt you were going to be a problem, they were going to solve it." The conversation ended quickly. They talked about his siblings and other things, and then she left.

A week later Detective Leyster showed up at Dahlia's doorstep. She had a distained look on her face because she knew why he was there. He handed her a subpoena to be in court for the prosecution. Angry, Dahlia said, "I ain't saying anything because I don't know anything. Didn't I tell your ass that man wasn't living here? How the fuck you going to ask me to help you, then you try to get me to talk about some shit I don't know? Get off my porch!" Grabbing the subpoena, she slammed her door. The detective was standing there looking at her like she was crazy. She grabbed her phone and called the prosecutor whose name was on the subpoena. The phone went to voice mail. The prosecutor's name was Ash. When it went to the beep, Dahlia lost it, blurting, "Look Ash, this is the mother of Talandas Heirloom, case number 245760098. I don't know what that detective told you, but I'm telling you, I ain't testifying against my son. I don't know anything. He is not and was not living here. If you choose to put me on the stand as a hostile witness, your ass will be sorry." She hung up. She felt she already turned him in, so that's all she was giving them. Anything else, they were on their own.

As the trial grew closer, her stomach, her very health was out of whack. Her urgency to puke or urinate was out of control. Killer's trial was starting the next morning. As usual, Dahlia prayed unceasingly. Dahlia loved the Lord and was worn out in prayer. Nevertheless, she kept praying. She felt certain she even prayed in her sleep. She prayed while she cleaned house, all day, every day.

That next morning in court, there were other trials and cases being heard. Dahlia gave Killer's lawyer his clothes for court. The jury had been selected, and the trial was on the way. Dahlia was able to sit in on all his other court dates, so she had a pretty good idea what had happened.

The first day of the trial Cecily went along. The prosecutor stood and spoke, "Your Honor, I have people here in the courtroom that are witnesses that need to be removed from the courtroom." The judge granted that. He began to call the names.

When he said Dahlia's name, she lost it. "Dude, didn't you get my message? I said I don't know nothing, and I ain't speaking against my son." Leaving the courtroom in anger, she found a seat on the bench in the hallway. When she raised her head, there she was staring at that Stover kid. Pissed off, she spoke firmly, "What you doing here? Your name came up little nigga. Why you ain't in jail? How the fuck you out here and they in there locked up? Your face was circled in that lineup. You did it, too. What the fuck you here, to be a snitch bitch? They are giving you immunity?" He got nervous and walked away. Dahlia sat there shaking her head saying to herself, I told that dumb ass kid of mine this motherfucker, Stover, was no good. He about to see.

Cecily was there in the courtroom. She was Dahlia's eyes and ears. The Stover kid was whisked away by the police. They kept him hid in the room for the witnesses. He never responded to Dahlia. She noticed his father wasn't there with him either. His testimony in this case was beginning.

That day, three people testified. It was the two victims

and the Stover kid. Once their testimony was over, Cecily rushed out and grabbed Dahlia so they could talk. Cecily whispered, "Girl, that little nigga, Rickey, got up there and told it all on everybody, girl! That nigga sat up there and said he was given immunity and that he didn't want to go to prison. He told how they robbed those two guys, and he told that it was Talandas, Dari, himself, Ugly Z, Mickey, and Mickey's little brother. They all got out the car, but only four pulled guns on the guys. It was two in the front, and two in the back of the victims. The witnesses said it was Killer, Rickey, Mickey, and ugly Z with the guns. They all held guns to those boys' heads and robbed them. Dahlia, it was horrible."

Dahlia was in a daze and spoke, "I knew they picked Talandas, Rickey, and Mickey out in a photo lineup, but, Rickey snitched on them?" Dahlia snapped. "You mean to tell me he talked to stay out of prison? I told Talandas that little nigga was no good. Now he a little snitch bitch."

When Rickey appeared, Dahlia saw him and she lost it, saying, "You little snitch bitch. I told my son you were no good. You robbed those young men too, and you walk, just because you snitched. I should crack your head, little nigga. You helping them send my son to prison when you where holding the gun to their heads too, man." Looking at the cops, Dahlia said. "How do you all sleep at night knowing you gave a person immunity when he was picked out in a photo lineup. You know he did it, too. You better hope he doesn't rob you or someone in your family." Walking away, she sat back on her bench and waited for the day to be over.

Court was released at four thirty and was due back the next day, which was Friday morning. Once everyone left the courtroom, Dahlia confronted the prosecutor, "So what you gonna do? I already told you I ain't testifying because I don't know nothing. Besides, I need to be in here with my son. I want to know what happened in those streets."

"Ms. Heirloom, I understand. I'll see you tomorrow." Shaking her head, she spoke again, "Look, you can't make me testify. Whether you use me tomorrow or not, I'm coming in here to be with my son. You can holler contempt of court or whatever." Storming out, she headed home. On the way home she cried like a baby, but that was nothing compared to what was to come tomorrow.

The next morning, Dahlia caught the prosecutor and asked him once again, "What you going to do?"

Looking at her, he asked her to come into the witness

room. He asked her the following questions with detective Leyster standing there and the snitch bitch sitting there.

"Ms. Heirloom, did you tell detective Leyster that your son had a gun?"

"No, I didn't tell him that. Dude told you a lie." She said it while looking right in the detective's face.

The prosecutor asked more questions. "Ms. Heirloom, do you know a Dari Mitchell?"

"I know of him. I can tell you this though; I didn't get a good feeling when I met him. I'd known he was trouble."

"Do you know a Mickey Crate?"

"I only saw him twice, when he brought my son by my house."

"Do you know what kind of car they were in?"

"Yes, an Escape."

"Do you know Mr. Stover here?"

She became angry.

"Yes, I know him, Mr. Immunity, huh? My son went downhill, running with Stover. He's nothing but trouble, and he should be on his way to prison, too."

"One more question, Ms. Heirloom, are you concerned about your son?"

"What kind of question is that? Of course I'm concerned about my son. Is there anything else, Mr. Ash?"

"No ma'am. You may be seated in the courtroom."

Dahlia walked in with the proper attire for Killer Kane to stand trial another day. He liked what his mom brought. Nine o'clock came, and the judge had arrived. She was an early judge. She was a no holds barred type judge, too. When the jury came in, Dahlia was feeling sick to her stomach, but she held on. When her son walked in, tears came to her eyes. She knew he could go away for the rest of his life, but she knew GOD had control and that wasn't going to happen. She was expecting at least 10 to 12 years if he was lucky. It bothered her that Mickey was allowed out on bail and was free all throughout the trial.

The prosecutor re-called one of the victims back to the stand. The line of questioning was frightening to hear. The prosecutor asked, "Roger, we questioned you about the robbery yesterday, and in your testimony you stated that there were four of them with guns to your head, two in the front and two in the back?"

"Yes, there were four of them."

"Can you please tell the court once again what

happened?"

"My friend, Milton, and I were walking up the street. It was around 9:30 p.m. The streets lights were just beginning to come on, and it was getting dark. As we were walking, we noticed a car that slowed down with their lights off, creeping past us. They flipped around on the opposite side of the street and they parked their car. My friend and I continued walking. When we saw them, we saw they were just kids, so we kept walking. They all crossed the street and began to walk towards us. Once two of them got past us, there were four guns drawn on us, two in the front and two in the back."

"Were you able to identify those that did that, and how?"

"Yes, by photo lineup."

"Who did you pick out in the photo lineup?"

"I picked Talandas Heirloom, Rickey Stover, Mickey Crate, and Koran Crate."

"What happened when they pulled their guns?"

"They instructed us to get on the ground, and they began to frisk our pockets. At first, we didn't go right on the ground, so they kept yelling to get on the ground, and Mr. Heirloom was the one with the gun to my forehead. While another one was in my back and the other two were on my friend with their guns, they were all laughing and joking about which one of us should get shot."

"If there were two in back and two in front, how did you see the other two that were behind you and your friend?"

"Once they got what they wanted, they told us to get up and walk away. I looked back and saw Mickey. The other two that were on my friend, I saw their faces when they walked past us."

"Thank you. That will be all, Roger." Both of the defense attorneys had the right to cross examine him, and they did. Mickey's attorney tried to make it seem like because the victims didn't see his braces, then it could have been anyone that fit the description. He thought that could create doubt for Mickey. It was over for Killer because the victim said he had the gun pointed to his forehead. Dahlia was glad they took a five minute recess because she had to puke. She couldn't believe her son was capable of such a thing. No mother wants to believe that. She thought these babies have lost their damn minds. These are babies out here robbing folks, violently. They are nothing but baby robbers. She knew those guys were bad news.

Throughout the trial that lasted two days, it was told. Mickey's little brother, Koran, was one of the baby robbers and so was a young man they called, Animal. It was six of them altogether. It was also revealed that there were more robberies, but they couldn't prove they did it, and they were running a car stealing chop shop rink, but the police couldn't prove that either. After Roger was re-called they called Mickey's dad to the stand. The prosecutor began to question Mickey's Dad, asking, "Mr. Crate, what city do you live in?"

"I live in Inkster, on Gloverhill and Barondale."

"Were both your son's Mickey and Koran together all day, that day?"

"Yes."

"Were they driving or walking?"

"They were driving."

"Whose car and what kind of car were they driving?"

"It was Mickey's car, and it was a Ford Escape."

"What color was the vehicle?"

"It is a dark blue color."

"Mr. Crate, do you know a Talandas Heirloom?"

"Yes, I know him because he and Mickey went to school together, and he would come to the house to visit, and I recall when his mom put him out."

"Back to your sons, and the day of the robbery. Did they arrive home together?"

"Yes."

"What time did your boys get home on June 19th?"

"They got home about 10:30 p.m. because that is their curfew on a school night."

"Mr. Crate, do you know a street called Pardon in Golden city, off of Gloverhill?"

"No, I do not."

"Well, Mr. Crate, are you aware, according to map quest, that it is less than a five minute drive from your home?"

"No, I am not."

"Mr. Crate, is Mickey's mom here in the court room today?"

"No, Mickey and Koran are adopted. I adopted them when they were little boys. I'm a single parent."

"Mr. Crate, do you own a gun?"

"Yes."

"Can you tell the courts what kind of gun you own?"

"I own a 9 MM glock."

"A 9 MM glock. Mr. Crate, are you aware that was one

of the weapons used in the robbery? No further questions."

Neither defense attorneys cross examined. Now, the arresting officers testified. It only took an hour to question them. Dahlia was ready for all of this to end. This was too much for her.

That Friday evening on October 22nd the jury deliberated on the case. Before they were released to deliberate, they were given their jury instructions. The jury came back without a verdict. That Stover kid was standing in the back of the court room with his head held high and a big grin on his face, looking at Killer. Killer just happened to look back and saw his boy, Stover, snitch bitch, standing by Dahlia, laughing at him. The one Talandas said would never snitch him out, but he did. Killer was so angry, he would have killed him in the court room.

It was 4:30 p.m., in the evening, time for everyone to go home. The deliberation was to start back on Monday. That was the longest weekend Dahlia had ever endured. That entire weekend she barely slept. Although she knew both of them were going to be found guilty, that wasn't what she feared. When they reached the hallway, Stover was running and playing. Dahlia gave him a look that could kill and said,

"Look here, young blood, you done gave your testimony, you laughing at my son like this shit funny. My son facing life and you should be, too, but I tell you what, don't come back up in here Monday. Your job is done snitch bitch, and if you do, I'm going to jail because I'm going to whip your ass like I'm your mammy."

She walked away in a fury. At that moment, she thought again. These kids are baby robbers. They're just babies out here robbing folks. What in the hell were those kids thinking? Driving home in shock, she had to pull over because the tears rolled down her face like a river. She began to pray this prayer: *Father, I come to you in the name of Jesus, first asking you to forgive my sins. Second, I ask that you spare my son that has gone astray because of his ignorance. Lord, you said, "Ask and you shall receive." Lord, I'm asking for mercy. I know he must pay for his crime, but Lord, his entire life is not what is required. Lord, I also would like to pray for the judge, that you will give her a heart of fairness and that you guide her in this harsh decision. I want to pray for all the other young men involved, that they may change and seek you first. Lord, I need not ask for a change in my son because I know this you will do if he is willing. This I pray in the of*

JESUS CHRIST, your son. AMEN."

Dahlia was more interested in the sentencing because she knew that would be the day her immediate family life would change. She was losing a son, Ripley was losing a stepson, and Tyler, Wood, and Valentino were losing their big brother. Dahlia sat the kids down often and talked to them about Talandas's problem and what he was facing. She expressed to them about what happens when you break the law and the consequences that follow. They understood, but they hated to see their brother go to prison. The house had a dark cloud looming over it for awhile. Nothing was ever going to be the same because now a family was torn apart by the streets.

Monday came. Dahlia showered, got dressed, and headed to court. It took the jury from eight in the morning until five o'clock in the evening to reach a verdict. Before they had reached a decision, the jury came back in and requested a playback of Roger's (one of the victim's) testimony.

At 5:00 p.m. the verdict was in. After the jury was seated, the judge asked, "Has the jury reached a verdict?"

"Yes, Your honor."

"Would the defendants please stand and face the jury?"

Dahlia knew by looking at Killer Kane that he was going to be fine, but she also knew that he knew he was guilty. Mickey thought he was about to get off.

The jury foreman stood and said, "We, the jury, unanimously find the defendant, Talandas Amid Heirloom, guilty of two counts of armed robbery, one count of felony fire arm, and one count of assaulting a police officer." Killer Kane stood there and just took the verdict. There was no emotion from him whatsoever, and that sent chills down Dahlia's spine. A person like that is a scary person to be around. Dahlia loved her son, but that was her honest feeling.

The jury foreman then read the verdict on Mickey. "We, the jury, unanimously find the defendant, Mickey Lance Crate, guilty of two counts of armed robbery and not guilty on felony fire arm." The Judge had a look of disbelief on her face and slouched back in her chair, as if to say, "Oh my God, I have to sentence these young men to prison."

Dahlia was angry. She couldn't believe that Mickey was not guilty on the felony fire arm charge. If there were four people, there were four guns. The judge allowed Mickey to go home until the sentencing date, but she warned him that he better return.

It was difficult for Dahlia to leave that building because she knew it would be awhile before she was able to be that close again to her son without a wall and a window. With tears in her eyes, she left thanking GOD for the blessing, the blessing of her son being alive and not dead. The way she saw it, he could have been killed and she could be burying a son. She had prayed that GOD would send him to prison verses the grave, and he answered. She knew that everything was going to be all right, but at the same time, she was a mother and a human being.

Dahlia had to return for sentencing in November. His sentencing was set for November 19th at 8:30 a.m. He was sentenced by noon. But, before he was sentenced, Dahlia wrote the judge a very touching letter, and in that letter she spoke the truth. She never tried to make light of her son's part in that crime. Dahlia had been thinking on this letter for awhile because at first she didn't know what to say to the woman who had her son's life in her hands, but she had to keep on living.

She went to visit Talandas that Monday after the guilty verdict. She was concerned about him trying to take his own life. She didn't know what was on his mind, but she was relieved to see he was okay. The visits with him continued to go on until he was sentenced. It was the longest three weeks ever. Ripley wanted to attend the sentencing, too.

Dahlia was sick, a nervous wreck. She lost weight, then gained, and lost it again. She was just all out of space on this ride. She held her breath until those three weeks came, it seemed. Even through her own pain, Dahlia continued to pray for Mickey and his father, as well. That kid's dad was torn apart, too. Those boys were going to be sentenced two days after Thanksgiving. There was sadness in Dahlia's house and in her heart. Her son was on his way to prison. She continued to visit her son faithfully. Some days she couldn't bare it, and she stayed home. She had her church, as a whole, pray for him. They knew Talandas. He was a member and still is. Believe it or not, Talandas was baptized, and that was a choice "he" made. Although he was running wild, GOD still had his hand on him the entire time. Dahlia was very grateful for that.

She took one day at a time and waited for the last dance, which was the sentencing. That day had finally arrived. Ripley and Dahlia were seated in court. They arrived at eight-thirty in the morning. 9:00 a.m. had rolled around. Mickey Crate's name was called, and there was no response. He wasn't there. Dahlia thought he skipped out, afraid of his punishment. 10:30 a.m. came and still no Mickey. One by one the prosecutor checked in, and then the defense attorneys came. Around ten thirty Mickey showed up in court. You could tell he was nervous and sick about this whole thing. He was sick even more so because he was no longer a free man; he was a prisoner.

The judge sentenced Mickey first. She scolded him very harshly. It was revealed he smoked weed, and the judge was angry about that. She scolded the father as well because he had the attitude of his son being innocent. The judge said to the father, "You know, Mr. Crate, what about the choices? I mean, you have said nothing of that sort." The Judge scolded Mickey a little more and sentenced him to two years. Dahlia was angry but sure that was bound to happen because the jury was too foolish to see the full truth. He only received a year for each robbery. After sentencing, he was taken into custody. He was no longer in the streets.

Then she moved on to Talandas. She took a pause, asking him if he was okay, and he responded, "Yes,"

She pulled out the letter Dahlia had written to her she said, "Mrs. Heirloom – Hilmar, I received your letter, and you have excellent penmanship, but that fails in comparison to the words you put on this paper. This letter kind of reminds me of my dad. If I were in trouble, this would be the type of letter he would write. Do you have anything to say before I sentence your son?"

Dahlia took a deep breath and said, "No, Your Honor, I think my letter says it all."

Looking at Talandas, she gave him a bit of a scolding but not like Mickey's. Talandas wasn't on any drugs, which Dahlia already knew. The judge asked Talandas what his plans and goals in life were. After his response, she sentenced Talandas to eight and a half years because he was guilty on all charges and the felony fire arm carried a mandatory two year prison sentence. Dahlia was crying up a storm, but on the inside she was thanking JESUS. Talandas was supposed to get at least a 20 to 30 year sentence. Heck, she could have given both of them letters, but she was lenient. Talandas was whisked back to the jail, waiting to be shipped out.

Dahlia visited her son in the Wayne County Jail until the day they shipped him out. He was there until after Christmas. She went to visit him on a Monday morning, but she had just missed him. They had just shipped him out. She knew where he was headed, to Jackson in quarantine for 30 days or longer. If you were there past 30 days, they were waiting on a spot for you. Dahlia knew he wouldn't be in the database for at least a week, then she would know where he was going to be for awhile.

They were all sent to the Chester E. Eggers Reception and Guidance Center in Jackson, Michigan. Killer was locked down there for at least sixty days. Gaither was Ugly Z's government name. He was there with Mickey and Talandas. He took a plea deal and received five years for his part in the crime. The other kid they called animal, Dahlia doesn't know how to spell his given name, but he is locked down, too. As far as Mickey's little brother who is a juvenile, still to this day, he walks the streets. The snitch bitch, Rickey Stover, still walks the streets, too. Killer Kane, after released from Jackson, was shipped to the Earl C. Banks correctional facility on level four. Gaither was shipped to the Hamlet Correctional Facility on a level two. Mickey was shipped to the Monroe Reform on level one, and as for Animal, Dahlia had not a clue. Mickey was supposed to be released December 2010. His father stated that he kept getting in trouble there, so he served an extended sentence, until he was paroled in 2011.

As Dahlia said, "Baby robbers are what they were." The baby robbers are now all on lock down, and Inkster is still off the hook. The baby robbers couldn't take the credit for that because they were silenced by prison cells.

To this day, Dahlia hopes and prays that her son will be rehabilitated and that he changes his ways because she knows after eight years in prison, if he gets out and goes back, that he will get letters, or death. All she can do is wait and see if her son has changed for the better when he is released in 2017.

In 2009, Killer Kane received DNA papers from the courts while in prison. DNA was taken, and it was established that he was the father of a baby boy. Dahlia takes her grandson to visit his father in prison, so he isn't a complete stranger to his son when he is released.

Killer Kane has been down three and a half years now, and time is moving fast. Dahlia is helping to raise Killer Kane's son until he is released. Talandas achieved his G.E.D. a year after his incarceration. It's a shame Talandas (Killer Kane) Heirloom had to go to prison to get an education. Guess that's what it takes for some folk to straighten out. Dahlia and Ripley support their son in prison.

In September 2011, Mickey was paroled. He received a

2 year 3 month to 10 year sentence. Ugly Z received 5 to 25 years. In the end Talandas had to serve the highest minimum but received the lesser tail, and Ugly Z had the highest tail of 25 years.

It's 2012 and Talandas has served 3 years and 9 months of his sentence. Mickey has been paroled. Ugly Z has served three years of his five year sentence. As to the other baby robber, it is unclear the amount of time he is to serve, the juvenile was not tried in the adult system, so his sentence was unclear.

www.ingramcontent.com/pod-product-compliance
Lightning Source LLC
Chambersburg PA
CBHW022115280326
41933CB00007B/402